and then there was one
Our journey from death to rebirth

written by
Margo and Matt Williams
during the year following Matt's suicide

Pooka Publishing Company
Sacramento, California

and then there was one
Our journey from death to rebirth

by Margo and Matt Williams

Published by:
    Pooka Publishing Company
    P.O.Box 19736
    Sacramento, Ca. 95816 U.S.A

Cover Design: Creative Factory, Sacramento, Ca.
Printed by: Griffen Printing, Sacramento, Ca.
Copyright 1996 by Margo Williams

All rights reserved, including the right to reproduce this book or portions thereof in any form, without permission in writing from the publisher, except by a reviewer who may quote brief passages in a review.

Library of Congress catalog card number:96-92372

ISBN: 0-9651897-0-8

This book is dedicated to those who
feel they can only "survive."

And to my son, who kept telling me
in so many ways his life had
not really ended, but was
transformed as he continued
his journey on a new path.

Acknowledgements

The year after Matt's suicide is pretty much lost to me. It is through reading our journal and talking with friends that memories and feelings converge. So if I have left your name off this list of caring, supportive friends, it is unintentional. You know what you did — please know you had an affect and you made a difference.

My sister, Sydnee and nieces Lorri, Lisa, Beth and Jamie. Friends Jim Hitte, Steven Smith, Barbara Hooker, Marilyn Brown, Suanne Carr, Gail Eatough, Myrle Rife-Helkenn, Wendy Horton, Alice and Charles Jasper, Terry Joyce, Inge, Darrell and Barbara Lindsey, Connie Mahoney, Bonnie Moore, Rae Ann Travis, and friends at Fair Oaks United Methodist Church.

Barbara Lindsey and Constance Warloe for advice and encouragement with the manuscript.

Sue Norwood and Gail Eatough for making the "magic" happen to bring it all together on the computer.

JOURNAL PROGRESSION:

Acknowledgements
Foreward: Loss by Matt Williams

Part One: Beginning?

The Premonition 15
Your Homecoming 23
A Plan Emerges 29
Keeper of the Memories....................................... 37
A Plan Revised 41
Spinning My Wheels 45

Part Two: The Great Conspiracy of the Living

Confusion.. 51
Survivors 55
Co-Author: Matt... 57
Is There A Me Without You?............................... 65
"Go There With Me".. 67
Leaving for the Last Time 73
Where is the Rule Book?..................................... 81
The Science Fiction Movie People...................... 87
Unwanted Life Support 91
Dead. Not Lost!.. 95
My Guiding Angel.. 99

Part Three: Searching

The Carmel River Woman 105
"Keep A Stout Heart!" 109
Burt's Shirts... 113
Life Renewing - Another <u>Why?</u> Question.......... 117
Mother's Day No Longer 123
This Poor Excuse for an Airplane 129
At the Bright Angel Hotel.................................. 133
Avalon 139

Part Four: Continuing!?

Without You 147
Moldy Tea 153
The Battle Continues, but the Fog is Lifting 157

Epilog: And Now?

Redefining Me.. 163

LOSS
by
Matt Williams

What is my real value?
Who is my true judge?
Am I a loser?
I think not.

I've lost a lot of people, places, and things.
I buried three "brothers" this summer
and one child.
I let a great job slip away,
and a wonderful girl.

Just when I thought it was all gone,
I had to look deep.
But I found something more.
A heart which is my most prized possession
because with every beat it makes the world
a better place.

Written in the fall semester of college 1994, a few months prior to Matt's suicide.

PART ONE:

. . . BEGINNINGS?

The Premonition

The pains of childbirth are not remembered. They join with other sensations and blend to be replaced with memories of a new life begun. Different is the pain of your death, and it is not fading away, but nearly consuming me. Is it because I was not with you at the end of your life as I was at the beginning?

You came into this life crying before you were fully out of my body. Then while you lay in a little bed with plastic sides, I watched as you looked all around with wide and knowing eyes, no longer crying, but seeming to take it all in – this challenge called life. I remember asking Dr. Elzey to hurry and finish with me so I could hold you, my precious son. Our journey together, however, really began prior to the evening of your birth of May 22, 1971. I felt our connection months before – knew you were a son and what your name would be – Matthew, gift of God. We had many talks, you and I. Knowing we would be alone, the two of us, on this life journey made our connection stronger. Our talks now are not unlike our talks prior to your birth. I was speaking to your spirit then as I do now. There is one great difference. The anticipation of our future together as mother and son no longer fills the conversations.

"Be my future, mom." – I hear your words. They fill my head as the tears of your passing fill my eyes. You were to be the future, Matt – I don't know how to be it for you. Show me. Somehow let me know what you want the future to be for me now, because I cannot envision being here without you. When the drugs took you into the closet, put the gun in your mouth and pulled the trigger, I also died. All that is left of me at this moment in my life is a living corpse that goes about performing daily tasks, talking, moving, unaware of much reality.

For me our journey's end began Friday, July 8th, sometime around 7:00 p.m. I was in the kitchen making plum jam for the church craft faire, secure in my belief that you had arrived back to your newly acquired flat in Ukiah on Tuesday evening, your truck overloaded with some more furniture and odds and ends from home. I knew you had to return to work Wednesday, and that you were awaiting a much anticipated vacation to Mexico later in the month with your friend Kevin. Your "Fourth of July" weekend back home in Sacramento had been hectic for you from the beginning – problems with your truck, many old friends to see, things to pack, drugs to do. Why the drugs again, Matt? You were so proud of being clean, having a job and succeeding in college – you had plans, you had *you* back.

The moment I heard your dad's voice on the phone I knew my dream from Wednesday night had come true – you were dead. All I remember of the dream was holding a box with your ashes in it and not knowing what to do with them. All I remember of Paul's call was his telling me you shot yourself and had died instantly. After hanging up I thought – Well

...Beginnings?

that's it then – knowing life was over. Others here were not aware of your passing. I did not want to tell anyone. It makes it real once you say it out loud. I began vacuuming the house and wandering from room to room, always ending up in your old room, not knowing what to do. Tears did not come. The grief experts call it shock. Finally I phoned my friend Jim who came over from his work. We talked and then I sent him home knowing he would be there if I needed him, but this was not about Jim and me. Next I called my pastor, Steve, and he came and then Judith. Phone calls were made, questions asked but not answered – why? how? when? The hardest part was telling your Aunt Sydnee. She and your cousins arrived. It must be real. They were all crying. You must really be dead. More questions – no answers. Still numb, I finally ask them all to leave. They do not go willingly, but I need this to end, to not be happening. They tell me they will be back tomorrow. Death keeps you very occupied at first. That night with you separate from this life was so frightening. I felt alone most of my life – before you were born – with one gun shot, I was back there again. Being in our house without you is not new for me – you have lived away for a while now. Being alive without you is unbearable.

    I began my journal writing July 10, 1994. Writing to you keeps you with me and I need that right now. Much of it is the rambling thoughts of a mother trying to make sense out of a senseless act. Mostly it has been a way through grief. It is my story, my rambling, my view of "reality" at the time.

and then there was one

July 10, 1994

I call your number many times during the day son, so I can hear your voice on the answering machine. How can you be dead – you are part of me and I am still here... mostly? The feeling of the last time we hugged and said goodbye is as clear as if it just happened (please God, let me have that for always). Did you really shoot yourself? Everyone says it is not possible. You promised me you would never do this. I talked with Paul tonight. He doesn't believe you shot yourself and wants more investigation done. I was told today by some of your friends that you were doing drugs all weekend. I just listen – all the information comes in and it feels like they are talking about someone else. If the final decision is that you shot yourself – I forgive you.

July 11

I miss being your mom. I want you back alive. How could this be happening? Today the doctor is doing an autopsy. Will you give us some answers that way? I have been planning a memorial service for people who love you. Your cousin Beth is going to sing to you and some members of your favorite Sacramento band, Filibuster, will play a song. Quite a divergent group of people love you, Matt.

It is night again. Sleep won't come. I try to talk to God. It used to be so easy and comforting. Now I just question and complain. Oh son, what will I do without you – who am I without you? I wrote this today:

...Beginnings?

God showed me in my dream –
I did not listen.
We are all very busy
        but Matt is dead.
The phone rings – don't bother me
I'm busy making jam
and it needs my attention
        but Matt is dead.
Vacation beckons – friends leave or are
already gone
        but Matt is dead.
Someone's child is ill, or leaving or not
living up to his potential
        but Matt is dead.
The apricots don't wait – they ripen anyway
and we need to pick them
        but Matt is dead.
I want to go dancing, laugh, make love,
feel again
        but Matt is dead.
Four thirty a.m. – the newspaper arrives
It is official – it says so in the obituary
        Matt is dead.
We who love you know differently
You are alive in our thoughts of you
Our laughter and tears
Our anger and pain
Our loving and caring
Connections – somehow we all become
a piece of each other – never to die.
        Matt is forever.

July 12

It is morning again, another day without you. I talked with Paul. The autopsy is over and they have already cremated your body. It is said that God won't give us more than we can handle – how strong does he think I am? This is too much. I am at the very edge. Paul talked with the police again. They believe you shot yourself. If it is true, I think your mind was taken over by the speed. Why did you take it again Matt and how do I forgive the young man you got it from?

Evening –
I've kept very busy today Matt, planning a memorial service for us – family and friends who miss you. I want to be with you. You were the best part of me. I feel so alone and empty – you were my future. I do not want to do it without you. Having you here kept me alive so many times in the past. How could I leave such a child as you – we were a team? When things got really sad and hard all I had to do was hold you or think about you. Does God think I am stronger now? Why did he take you so soon? You were just beginning, now I am ending – and it is taking too long.

July 13

I went to see Joseph today to order flowers for Saturday. They are not going to look like funeral flowers; they will be very special just for you. I feel like I am kind of floating – disconnected.

...Beginnings?

July 14

This is the day your grandpa died so many years ago. You were only six years old when you gave him his last hug before the ambulance took him to the hospital. Then Grandma died six months later. My new job and the numbness of grief took me away too for a time. You endured too many losses during your life, son.

I spent most of today numbed out – not feeling. Your friends had a get-together tonight and asked me to come over. Jim went with me. We stayed for a short time. It was very difficult to be there. I kept wondering why you and not one of them? How did they escape? Deep inside I knew you were in trouble again with the drugs. As usual, I stayed quite comfortably in denial instead of helping you. I hate not being your mom anymore. I do not want to do this.

Paul brings your ashes to me tomorrow. I want to be in the box with you.

and then there was one

℘Ⴒ
Your Homecoming

July 15

a.m.
You are coming home today son. I hear you saying "I'm home already mom." I often feel you with me and sometimes feel that you are other places.

p.m.
Taking that box containing your ashes was the second hardest thing I have ever had to do. Listening to Paul tell me on the phone that you shot yourself was the hardest.
The box was much heavier than I expected. It had no weight in my dream. Paul, Susan and Nate plan to create a memorial spot for you on their property. They probably want to take you there. You are going to have to let me know what you want, son. Right now I just want you here. I held you most of the day. Fell asleep later in the rocking chair with you in my arms. Crazy-making, this death stuff.

July 16

Your memorial service was today son. Joseph fixed lovely flowers with ferns and other greens – you would have approved. They were not "funeral flowers." You know everyone who was there because you were there too. I think you are with your friends right now. That's okay – I am so tired. I am going to be with Jim for a while. It is different energy at his flat. He is separate from my life with you, and I need to be away from our home for a little while. When I am here, I miss you so much. It feels like the edge of insanity and any minute I will be in the grip of it. A few weeks ago I remember feeling so complete and thinking for the first time "maybe I could even live and go on if Matt was not in my life" – the part about being able to go on without you – it was a lie. I see no future unless you are in it. I see day after day after day, but not a future.

July 17

This morning Jim took me to Auburn to see the Biblical Gardens. It is a beautiful and peaceful place. I am very lucky to have his friendship. He has been a resting place for me.

I am home now son, sitting on the patio and watering the lawn, thinking of you. Life without Matt, without connection to a human being that is part of me. People ask me how I am doing. My body is okay but my spirit has been beat up, and is all bruised and bleeding.

...Beginnings?

July 18

I had another dream last night. I felt you with me and a very odd thing happened. Our cat Tiger came into the bedroom, jumped up on the bed and lay down on my back. He began purring very loudly and became quite heavy. I was awake and still in the dream all at the same time. It felt like you were coming to me through him to hold me. The cat has never done this before. In fact I was sure I had put him outside before going to bed. He lay on my back for a while and then went to the foot of the bed where his blanket is and fell asleep. I felt very comforted. There won't be many I can tell this to. Most will think I'm losing it for sure!

July 20

I have stopped feeling. I guess my spirit needs a rest. I am physically just going through the motions of living. People are more comfortable with me this way. Aunt Sydnee sees through me, so do Barb and Jim. I'm worried about my sanity, but as long as I am worried about it I guess I haven't totally lost it. Everything seems so temporary to me. You would think it would all mean so much more because of this loss of you. Actually it has the opposite effect. Getting up doesn't even seem important. I eat about one meal a day, and that is if I go out with someone. I have to find the energy to get the house cleaned up and in order. I do not want to do this much longer.

July 21

This has been a very hard day Matt. I miss you so much. Why did you leave me? Twenty three years is not long enough to be a mom. I wanted to be a grandma and spoil your babies. There won't be any babies now. You had no right to kill my son – didn't you know how much I would miss you? Oh Matt, I want to die too.

July 26

I have been to Tahoe with Jim. He took me to visit his sister Connie and her husband Ed. They have a cabin at the North Shore. The weekend was a good distraction and being with Jim is so comfortable and safe. Once back in Sacramento and after he went home I was alone again and I felt so empty. I do not feel you around me – is it because I have stopped feeling? I can just sit for hours. I hear and see things – sometimes I even react and carry on a conversation, but I am not really there. It is okay with Jim. He accepts me the way I am. I ended up calling Barb very late and driving up to stay at her house.

July 27

You were in Philo most of the day. Your dad and his family had another Memorial Service for you there. I didn't go. I do not belong there. When this is all done, I don't want to see or talk to Paul anymore. Sorry Matt, it is the way I feel right now. He will be bringing the rest of your things home tomorrow. I

...Beginnings?

have been cleaning out your closet. I found two letters you wrote to me. Well they were not really letters. You were venting some very angry feelings (about age 18 or so). No matter what I said or did you never believed how great you were. I am sorry for all the things I did not do or say correctly. I have been living in the land of "if only" lately. It is not much fun and very painful. Then I remembered what you told me a year ago on Mother's day when we were sitting on our patio. Did you somehow know then time was short and you needed to tell me those loving and wonderful words that helped to heal our mother/teenager relationship? I know I thanked you and told you how much hearing them meant to me. But I did not hear all you were saying – under the heartfelt words you were also expressing how sad and hopeless you felt. I did not hear that part – or did not want to. I am sorry I was not enough to keep you here. Jim says we all do the best we can with what we know, that I did just what I was supposed to do, we all did. Including you. There are no accidents, right son?

July 28

Paul and your brother Nathan brought me some more of your belongings, but all I want is you. I held your box of ashes today and rocked you for a while – yes, your old mom is losing it! I know you are not in there. I just want to hold you. I have had this feeling for months – way before you died. The need to hold you and touch you while there was still time.

Paul and I had a long talk today. He is feeling very sad and guilty about many things. I let him have his feelings and thanked him when he apologized for leaving us before you were born. That is his stuff to deal with. I released the pain of it for me a long time ago. Forgiving the pain it caused you is none of my business.

I was not able to tell Nate the things you wanted me to tell him. They left before I returned from picking up Mrs. Currie from the visit with her husband at the hospital, so later that night I wrote him a letter for you.

It is 11:30 and I am very tired. Falling asleep is difficult. I hate that you were in that dark closet, son. I see you there when I close my eyes. My pastor, Steve, says you were not there for long. A white light came instantly and took you from the pain. What about the pain that put you in there? How long had that been with you? I am sorry I was not there, son.

A Plan Emerges

July 29

I did not know you, my son. I did not know your pain. I sit reading your poems and writings – getting to know you, my grown son, a bit more. I clung too tightly to the child I knew so well, afraid to know the young man completely. Not able to reach through the anger and fear I had helped create. It is too late now. You ended any chance I might have had to make amends. To face the truth of us and build life from there. You left your pain and fear with me. It is too much – I cannot bear it.

July 30

A respite. Jim came for dinner and for me. I felt alive for a brief time, and then reality crept in after he had gone. There is no you anymore.

July 31

I felt you here tonight, sitting on the couch. We talked of time and how it is different, non existent where you are. Forever – no beginnings and no ends. On this plane we measure time in seconds but you asked, "What about the time between the seconds? You see it can't really be measured – no beginning, no end."

Dear God, please bring something to replace this sadness inside me that fills the place where my son used to live.

Aug. 1

Sydnee, Lorri and Beth came for dinner tonight. We were talking about Jamie and her baby Andrew. We know they need help, but we cannot seem to agree on an answer. I wish I could ask you. I know you have feelings about being raised by a single mom. I cannot help wondering if you would still be alive if I had let you be adopted. If I had, I don't think I would be.

Aug.2

I woke up this morning feeling nearly normal, without the horrible sadness. It did not last long. I called the mortuary to find out about your autopsy. The tests are still not completed and your death certificate is not ready. They will not put the day of your death as July 7th. They say they must put it the day your body

...Beginnings?

was found. I do not know why this angers me so. Perhaps because it feels like one more way you have been discounted in your life. I am sorry, son.

Aug. 3

Norbert Currie died today, Matt. I was with him. I was with Grandpa and I was with Grandma when they died, but you, my precious child, were alone. I cannot bear it. I am losing my mind. On the outside I go on. People think everything is fine with me. I am "courageous and holding up well." It is a sham. I do not want to be here, Matt.

Aug. 4

I began a drawing class tonight and am going to Kathy's cabin tomorrow. School begins in three weeks. Don't they know you are dead? Everything just goes on as if it doesn't matter. It matters!

I have decided if I take one room at a time to clean and get ready, the task won't be so overwhelming. Maybe I can get done before school begins. I have another mess there to sort out. Probably by the end of September I can be with you. It is what keeps me going son. People will be sad for a while, but soon they won't notice I'm not here, either.

Aug. 5

I am up at Echo Lake in Kathy's cabin. It is very late and I have awakened from a dream about you. All I recall is your saying "She thinks there was just one, but there were three." I have no idea what this means. It has been a day filled with tears and longing for you. I seem to get very emotional just before a trip. Maybe leaving the house means leaving you – although I felt you with me on the drive up...giving driving instructions, of course!

The death of you stands for the reproach of all my sins and a reminder of all there is to lose in life at any instant. It is the loss of everything – of hope, of life, of future. It is also the loss of the present. How do I stay here when I want so much to go back in time when you were with me?

Aug. 7

Leaving home is difficult. Returning is terrifying. How can everything look the same when nothing feels the same? I enter our house and instantly know you are no longer part of this. Grandpa and grandma built the house for me and Aunt Sydnee. I bought it after they died and have made it your home. You were supposed to inherit it to do with as you saw fit. Now it means nothing to me.

...Beginnings?

Aug. 8

My mind dwells lately on all the negative words and actions that came from me when I was your mother. I am haunted by the belief that if I had told you more often how great you were, done so many things differently, you would still be alive. As I was sitting in the car today, the thoughts returned. This time you interrupted and told me how you understand now – clearer even than I do myself. You know the whys of everything that happened to you, whether by me or someone else. You see, understand and forgive. You asked me to believe you. To have faith. I often wondered in our relationship as mother and child who was raising whom. You always seemed to have so much insight and wisdom, from little on. Until the drugs Matt – there lies the biggest failure, my denial about your drug use.

Aug. 9

The toxicology report came in. You had alcohol and speed in your blood. There were so many who would have been there for you, Matt. You chose the drugs. I want you alive, son – you are missed so much by so many people. I just wrote to your friend, Kevin, and sent him a copy of the paper you wrote for school about the upcoming trip to Mexico you two had planned. He, too, is devastated and confused by your choice to die.

and then there was one

[English class , Spring semester, Ukiah Community College]

Mexico
by Matt Williams

    I finally have something to look forward to. This summer I'm going to Mexico! My buddy Kevin and I are going to drive his RV to Ensenada, (I think that's how it's spelled) and camp on the beach for two weeks. I'm finally going to be in an environment so economically depressed, I'll feel wealthy. I can go to markets and buy whatever clothes I want. Bars will be great too. For the first time I'll be able to leave decent tips. If I get the chance, I want to check out some Maya or Aztec temples. (I'm not sure which lived in that region).
    The best part will be the beach. I love the ocean. Lounging on the beach with a Margarita in one hand, my notebook open in my lap, and a fishing pole in the other will do wonders for my sanity. With no distractions from friends and neighbors or school and work I can probably get some good writing done. Ever since reading "On the Road" by Jack Kerouac I've always wanted to go to Mexico. It would be great if I could write like him, Hunter S. Thompson and Ernest Hemingway all rolled into one. I could be a man of nature and the first drug-free gonzo journalist at the same time.

...Beginnings?

Aug. 10

Tonight I was ready to join you. I was sitting in the rocking chair, just sitting, not feeling anything except the need to end this emptiness. I wrote this letter to everyone I love and would leave behind:

> Please forgive me, but I cannot stay
> My feelings of pain and emptiness are
>   greater than my need to live.
> You all helped me and did as much as
>   I would allow.
> I do not want to heal from this. I do not
>   believe it is possible.
> People say I was a good mother to
>   Matt and I do not know why they do.
> The evidence has proven them wrong.
> The pain that led to Matt's death
>   was not a stranger to me.
> I knew of it.
> I chose not to believe anyone as
>   wonderful and bright as he would
>   be defeated by it –
>   now I understand.
> Please forgive me, but I cannot stay.
>   I love you,
>   Margo

It was about 10:00 and the phone rang. It was Mrs. Currie from across the street. She had left her medication in my car (I took her to the drugstore today). I brought it over to her. We hugged, we talked, we cried. Why didn't you talk to someone son? What was so awful you needed to end our lives?

Aug. 11

I woke up about 4:00 and read the paper and went back to sleep until 10:00 and later took a two-hour nap. I accomplished nothing today except to write a letter to your English teacher, Sharon, go to my drawing class and visit Jim – he has been a refuge in this storm.

Keeper of the Memories

Aug. 13

I received the coroner's report today. I took it over to Jim and he read it. I do not want to read it son – I am struggling to remain sane with what I know. If I read the official report describing your death, I will surely go completely mad. I want to rent a large dumpster and empty the house of everything that is you and me. It is so painful to be in this house without you.

Aug. 15

I go back to work next week, Matt. I am so scared and I am not even sure why. Part of it is because not all of me will be there. When I look at myself in the mirror, I see a dead person in a body that is still breathing, moving, functioning. Most adults cannot tell, but the kids will know. I am hoping I can fill up again with their extra energy. I took Kyle to the zoo and "Humpty Dumpty Land" today – remembered you at three and how much life you brought to everyone you were with and everything you did. Do you think I am going to make it son? Do you think I am going to live? I still don't want to.

Aug. 16

You hid so much from me Matt and yet I knew you well – or as well as I was meant to. I miss you, son. I wanted to know the rest of you. I wanted our life together to be longer. I don't know if I am coming to you, son. At first I thought I would. I wanted to join you. As the days go on I am not so sure anymore. What I hear you telling me is your choice was yours – it does not have to be mine.

I was able to pray tonight, not just words, but with my heart, for the first time since you died. I asked what to do about the part of me, the huge black space that you lit up, and was told to surround it with the light and love of all the children I would be teaching. I asked for the strength to let you go and asked that you visit when I need you. I am so grateful for having had you in my life, even for the short time. If I kill myself, son, then you will truly be gone from this earth. I am in charge of keeping your memory alive. You are alive inside me forever.

Aug. 19

Tonight as I was meditating and questioning and complaining I told God that I wanted so much to let him heal my broken heart and to feel his presence

...Beginnings?

within me again. I am so angry, Matt, and so ashamed of the anger. You told me to write to God like I write to you and answers would come. I will give it a try, son.

Dear God,
Were you in the closet with Matt? [Yes Margo – I took his spirit in my arms as soon as he released it from his body. You have asked me many times to hold him close so he would come to know me. We have a long relationship, Matt and I. His lessons were hard this time and he learned them well. In his dying he taught you things you needed to learn.] I might choose to die too – to end my life. [It is your choice.] I am very angry with you. [I know.] It feels not only that I lost Matt, but you, too. [I am here – you know many answers but you have not been listening to yourself. Accept that you need to rest and you do not have to "heal" and "be done with it" so soon. You have time. Allow the process to happen. Be aware of the connections. I am with you.]   Thank you.

Aug. 20

I read the coroner's report tonight son. I am still alive, sitting here in bed wearing your leather jacket. It has your scent and I feel close to you. It is often beside me or in my arms as I fall asleep. Reading the report has rendered me numb again. My spirit has receded deeper into that black empty space. For now, I will curl up in your jacket and sleep. I hope you will be in my dream time tonight. Morning is always easier after you have visited. I love you.

and then there was one

A Plan Revised

Aug. 23

You have a new second cousin, Matt. Lisa gave birth to a little girl at 11:24 tonight. What a miracle it was seeing that little soul being born; she came to this life with eyes wide open, as you did. She was born thirty three minutes before your time of birth. I want you here so we can celebrate the birth of your babies some day. You tell me that you are with the little baby you lost to a miscarriage. Hold her close son and keep her little spirit with you until I join you.

Aug. 25

I have been back to school this week preparing my classroom for the start of another school year. No matter what people say, it does not help to "keep busy." I have no energy for living. All I want to do is be somewhere alone with nothing to do or think about. I want to go into a dark closet and disappear, like you did. I am back to thinking about ending my life. November will be the right time. I just want to be with you, Matt. There is nothing left inside me anyway. I was filled with me and you. Without you, there is no me.

My soul is buried deep inside that blackness and my spirit just sort of floats around me looking for you. When I look at myself in the mirror, I do not recognize that person. It is like looking at a confused, lost stranger.

Aug. 28

I made it through the first day of school. I did not let myself think about you until after school. This would have been your first day back to college, too, Matt. You had already registered for classes. The continuation of your new plans. You were so proud of your last semester's work. Paul told me you were on the Dean's list. You had plans to transfer to Humboldt State. How can the world survive without people like you? I did not tell you often enough how wonderful and meaningful your life was. I am feeling so much guilt around your death. I need to hold you, son.

Sept. 4

I am not sure why I have stopped writing. Mostly I am either numb, confused, tired or all three at once. Working is more difficult than I thought it would be. It is most difficult driving to school and coming back home.

This Labor Day weekend I have gotten a lot of

...Beginnings?

things cleared out at home. There is much more to do. It is 2:30 and I am going to sleep now. Come to my dream time, son.

Sept. 5

Cleaning out closets and drawers is going too slowly. There is so much to do. I cannot leave this mess for Sydnee and the girls. School again tomorrow. Why do I feel so afraid? I have been having panic attacks more often. In the restaurant today I went in to order a little bit of food, but could not decide and ended up with four different items. Then I sat down to eat, but there were too many people. I had to leave. I cried all the way home. How can I teach my class when I can't even order lunch?

Sept. 6

A pretty good day today Matt, no panic attacks and I was able to write lesson plans for the rest of the week. Not an easy task anymore. My concentration and attention to details are gone. I talked with a friend after school. She is worried about my depression – wants me to call a psychiatrist and maybe get on some medication. I don't know. I guess I could talk with someone about these feelings. I do not like the confusion and panic attacks, but do not think medication is what I want either. I just need you back, son. One little miracle, that's all.

and then there was one

Sept. 11

I will be going to Burlingame October third to take a grief class – so I can do it "right" I guess. I have decided against the medication. It is not what I am supposed to do right now.

During these past few days I have been detaching from you son. You need to leave with your spirit guides and go on. Detaching does not mean forever. You have things to learn about and then you can come back to visit me. This was told to me during meditation. It makes sense, but the numb, empty feeling is back with me. Sometimes I go on for days like this and then it hits me – you died, you really died. You are not in Ukiah and you will not be calling or coming home for a visit. You are no more, and I am fading.

Sept. 14

I felt you with me this morning while driving to work. Enormous sadness came over me. Then tonight during my meditation you were there. This time with numerous guides and angels. They were telling us that you needed to go with them for a while. You were very sad. You wanted to you stay with me. I want that too, but I know you must go on to continue your work. I did not think it would happen so soon and am very confused.

Spinning My Wheels

Sept. 18

Confusion has turned to sadness and anger. I do not feel Matt's spiritual presence here anymore. I believe it will return after a while. Questions – Do I stay? If I stay, how do I live without him? I feel empty and am not pleasant to be around. My grieving seems to be happening during my dream time more than my awake time. The awake time is filled with thoughts of anger and uselessness. Not a pretty sight. If I continue journaling, do I write to Matt as before, knowing he is gone? Do I write at all?

Sept. 25

I never seem to be able to catch up with all that needs doing. Am I staying in this confused, never-getting-anything-completed state of mind because I know once everything is in order I will really need to decide whether to live or die? Curious.

I have written the letter I will leave to everyone

who wants to read it. I wrote it on August 10th. It still applies. Intellectually I understand that I am supposed to live. I am loved, needed, worthwhile, but in my heart and soul I feel empty and sad and I long for closure to this pain. I am sorry for the sadness and pain I will cause by dying, but have seen that is really does not last too long. People hardly speak to me of Matt anymore. It will be the same with me. We both made a difference while we were here. Life will go on, and rightly so, when we are gone.

I believe it is possible to fill that black empty place inside that is left when a parent dies, or a husband or brother or sister; but the void left by a child, never. It fills up with tears until you drown.

Oct. 1

"Any bullet from wherever it comes is shot at the mother first, not at the son who is killed." I read this in a book today. The quote was written by Van Le, a Vietnamese poet and novelist. It feels true.

Oct. 3

Sydnee, Beth and I went to Burlingame today to a grief workshop. It brought up a lot of anger for me and frustration. It seems there are rules and stages to this grief work and I am in the midst of one that is not on the list. The leader said that in order to heal we must go through the stages. I do not even see the possibility of healing from Matt's death. I see no future and am growing very tired of the present.

...Beginnings?

Oct. 9

My neighbor, Jane, had a wedding shower today for Jackie. Matt was to be Tony's best man at the wedding in November.

Kyle had his fourth birthday party. All of Sydnee's grand babies were there. Well not Lorri's girls, but all the little ones.

I met with an old friend after church. She did not know about Matt's suicide. Another time of "reliving" his death.

This was not my favorite day. I am filled with anger. I want out of this nothingness.

and then there was one

> # PART TWO:

The Great Conspiracy of the Living

and then there was one

Confusion

Oct. 11

I feel so empty. Writing in this journal brings no comfort or release of pain as it did when I was writing to Matt. Three months have passed. It feels like it just happened – Matt is dead. Everyone's love and caring do not penetrate the empty void that was my son. Please understand – <u>I do not want to be here without him.</u>

Oct. 22

I keep putting myself in situations where what I choose depends on whether I am going to live or not. Like when I was at Lorri's craft faire today. Do I buy this or that to redecorate the house or forget it?

The washing machine broke. Now do I go to the Laundromat or invest in a new washer and dryer that no one will need when or if I am gone?

Nov. 1

I have begun writing to you again Matt, because I have begun feeling your presence once more. You have been gone a little over a month, and have returned to me in a different way. I do not have words to explain it now.

The afternoon was spent attempting to clean out the garage. Floods of memories. It has been my garage for thirty-nine years! Much of my time was spent here in my youth and yours. You left a lot of "stuff" for me to deal with, Matt – books, clothes, engine parts, exercise equipment I cannot even lift. If the getting-angry-at-you part of grieving ever comes out, the garage will probably be the catalyst. But not today. Only sad feelings of missing nagging you about your messes and guilt feelings around ignoring the drugs you probably did while spending time out here.

I wanted to be the mom you needed. The person who could lead you through the confusion of your teenage years. Instead I was frozen in my fear of all that was happening to the child I cherished and understood for so long. Unable to admit you were growing beyond the boy with simple hurts I could fix with a hug and kiss. Questions denied – not wanting to know the truth. Why were you so unsure of your worth, so empty of the wondrousness of you that you filled the empty space with drugs? Getting gratification from them instead of from inside yourself? I felt helpless and alone. Not knowing how to reach that part of you. How to tell you so you would hear me, really hear me – you are enough as you are. I want the pain of it to stop. I want to die, too. This life with-

The Great Conspiracy of the Living

out you – I am not enough without you. Please, God, let the beating that remains in my broken heart, and the meaninglessness of my life stop, too.

and then there was one

Survivors

Nov. 2

I went to a meeting for survivors of suicide tonight. I haven't survived – have no belief that I will survive. I don't even want to survive.

As I enter the room the greeter says, "It's good to see you here." I reply to Beth, who accompanied me tonight, "Why is it good? If I am here, doesn't that mean someone I love killed himself?" I sign the registration, put on my name tag and go in. There is no energy, no true energy in this room. The people who lead the meeting, the ones in charge of surviving, have an appearance of the "surviving thing," but I see inside them and they still have not filled the empty space that used to make them complete.

It is time to introduce ourselves. I listen. There are so many people, but it is only me and it is only each one of them that this has ever happened to. The numbers do not count. We are each the one and only in our own pain.

I leave early, leaving behind the "uplifting poem" that was so lovingly offered.

As we drive home I question, getting angrier with each mile, why I was supposed to be there. What was the lesson? Then I realize this has been another opportunity to feel the anger. I do not want to be a suicide survivor. I won't be. Who says I have to survive? And then there was that family of women all sitting around the table next to ours, comforting each other in their loss. I saw the future. My sister and nieces sitting there after I leave this life. I will be making them "survivors of suicide." Everything that happens lately is conspiring to keep me here in this life. I want to shout at the top of my voice. STOP. LET ME GO. LEAVE ME ALONE. I DO NOT WANT TO DO THIS ANYMORE!

Nov. 3

Reflections of "the meeting" last night:

Shrouded in our personal experiences we are as little islands, clustered together in a sea of despair. Close, feeling the same waves of numbness and pain. Not able to touch – really touch the soul of the other. We are labeled "survivors" with common bonds, though we do not really know each other's grief. Bonded only by the tragedy of unexpected death.

Co-Author: Matt

Nov. 6

Today you have been dead four months. How can this be? Where was I all this time? It is as though I just got the phone call confirming my prophetic dream. Instead of getting easier, everything is becoming more and more difficult. How much longer can I go on, split apart – teacher, friend, sister, aunt, grieving mother. Each one separate. Each needing, no required to behave a certain way, depending on the circumstance. The grieving mother surfaces more and more often. I am so tired of maintaining the pretense of "surviving", doing my job, being who I am expected to be.

Nov. 9

While sitting in the hair salon I observe a young man getting his hair cut. You will not be doing that any more, Matt. A new Star Trek movie is coming, and Stephen King just released a new book. Why do they bother? Don't they know you are dead? You are not here to do all the things that gave you pleasure, yet these things keep happening; keep reminding me of the finality of your death.

The wound that began in my mind and heart when I learned you took your life is getting larger and deeper. I am often fooled into thinking it is healing a bit. Then I see a young man doing what you will never be doing again, or pass through the men's department of Macy's and tell myself how great this or that would look on you. I go to buy it. Then remember once again you are no more, and whatever suturing that has taken place on my wounded heart and soul breaks apart.

Will the tears ever stop? Today it came to me why I am so tired all the time. It takes an enormous amount of energy to hold the tears inside, do my job, be strong and courageous. These adjectives, strong and courageous, have defined me most of my life. It is not working any more. This is no longer who I am and I am weary of keeping up the pretense, yet do not recognize the replacement either.

Nov. 13

Your jacket surrounded me as I left our home heading for Richardson Springs Retreat. Tears and panic accompanied me. This is my M.O. when I leave home for more than a day. It is as though I lose you all over again each time I depart. I cry every day on the way to work with the sadness of leaving the energy of you that remains in our home, and on the way home with the knowledge that you will never be there again.

Nov. 25

Thanksgiving is past. The first holiday without you. I planted bulbs in our garden, watering them with tears from missing you.

Nov. 26

I have begun a new method of communicating with you son. It is called automatic writing. I write questions and before the answers can formulate in my brain, my hand begins writing. Forming words that do not come from me but through me. It is you in spirit. This is my belief.
Are you okay? (*Sometimes it's hard here because I feel sad about what I did to you, leaving the way I did. Mostly there is lots of love. It's the way to understand the lessons – through the love. It opens the mind to knowing. I still have much to learn.*) **I want to be with you. Living without you is too hard.** (*I am with you mom. The way I'm supposed to be. Wait, ask and listen. You will know what to do.*)

Nov. 27

I am going to Ukiah, to the closet where you shot yourself Matt. (*I'm not there. My energy is gone. You will only feel your own pain. You can feel that at home. You saw my place, mom. You helped me find it. I loved it. It wasn't all of me in the closet. It was the insecure, drug user. I'm sorry he won. I miss you. I'm with you. You don't need to go there .*)

I want to remember my dreams I have with you in them, Matt. (*You will remember the feelings if not the exact details. I'm with you mom, hang in there.*) I am hanging – by a thread. I do not want to be here without you. (*The answers are not only with me. They are inside you, just listen.*) The tears get in my way. (*So do the alcohol and pills.*) You are a fine one to talk. (*I see it all clearer from here.*) I don't care anymore. I don't want to live. (*I don't believe you.*)

Dec. 6

Five months into the abyss. Days come and go. Disappear as if they never were. I do what is necessary – work, eat, grieve. Why? Why is it December and I am still here when I had planned to stay only until November? I still have not completed all the tasks I must do before leaving. No will is written, closets are not cleaned out, belongings not given away. Has anyone but Jim, Beth, Bonnie and me been in our house since the week you died? There are still many of the same things in the living room that were there the night I got the phone call about your death. A pitcher of tea made for visitors in July molds in the refrigerator. Why don't I throw it out? Why haven't I put away your school papers Paul brought me, or the remaining memorial service programs? Why haven't I put me away?

Matt, this is going to sound very strange. Do you come to me in the middle of the night through our cat Tiger? Every night at about the same time, he comes up from his blanket at the end of the bed and gets right next to my neck and begins purring and touching

The Great Conspiracy of the Living

my face with his paw. This is not at all like our independent, don't touch me, thank you very much cat. (*It is me mom. I miss you and I love you.*) Why don't I dream about us any more? (*Your mind is not clear enough. Stop taking the pills and alcohol.*) **No.** (*Use your prayers to get to sleep, like you used to do.*) My prayers always were around you and my thankfulness for you in my life. And that you were back in school and happy – I thought. What do I pray for now? (*That you will come back.*) NO! Don't you get it, Matt – I do not want to BE HERE (*Well, guess what, you are.*)

This lesson is too much to survive. Living takes more energy than I have. I slept almost all weekend. I like being asleep more than being awake.

Eight more days until Christmas vacation. A new decision to make – I will go on until July. July is a good time to die. Right, son? (*Very funny mom.*) I am getting very good at making people believe I am okay. (*It comes with years of practice.*) Now I know where you learned it.

Jim and I are disconnecting. This is good. It will make leaving easier. My curiosity about life is my enemy. Wondering what will happen in the future to all the ones I care about. Am I supposed to be a part of it? Will it make a difference if I am not? No one's life would be drastically altered by my death, as mine was by yours. (*Take another look.*)

Dec. 8

A closeness is growing between my nieces and me since your death son. They have always been a great source of love and pride. It grows as I come to know each as an adult. We are able to talk now as equals – friends. They have seen me vulnerable and comforted me and I in turn have listened to them and from somewhere – from you perhaps – have helped them find some of the answers they seek.

Tomorrow I will stay home from work and do some resting. I am too weary to face work another day. The kids deserve better. A parent of one of my students called, complaining. I did not need to hear it today and she would only talk, choosing not to listen to anything I said. There are so many frightened young parents without a clue what to do, yet sure they have all the answers. It is very frustrating to have the knowledge and insight I have after twenty years of teaching and not be able to reach them. (*They will "get it" when they are supposed to. Don't give up on them, either.*)

Dec. 9

Your pictures hang on the walls, reminders of my great fortune and great loss. Each time I see your photograph my heart stops a beat and my throat tightens, holding back the sobs. Memories of times passed and awareness of times never to be. Your baby and little boy pictures are easy to look at. That child was supposed to grow up and leave, making his way and opening up new possibilities. The pictures of my son, the young man, tear at my soul. This should not be the end, not be happening. Something is very wrong. A great mistake has been made. More rambling of the grieving mother.

and then there was one

Is There a Me Without You?

Dec. 12

The friends that have remained near me in these last months are also grieving. Some for dead loved ones, others for changes in their lives or for the person they thought they were. For sons moving out or onto college, for divorce, or pending retirement. Do they accept me and my pain because it is not a stranger to them? For whatever reason I am still here because of them.

I began writing this journal, Matt, to be close to you, to sort out my thoughts and feelings – to remember. Now it goes beyond this. Journaling is not only about keeping you with me. It is also about beginning to know who I am without you. This thought came to me after discovering a note I had written to God. In it I asked what the missing part is that will keep me alive? The answer came to me in these words: time, Matt's writings, love, knowing who you really are completely.

Will there be a complete me without you? Is it possible? Perhaps living or dying is not dependent on how much I love you, son.

Dec. 13

There comes a time when "letting go" of someone you love is essential to holding on to life. What will be my way of "letting go?" Will I even attempt to discover it? If in the discovering, you are no more once again, what then? There are many victims when someone commits suicide – least of those the one who dies. I have always believed it to be the most selfish thing a person can do. But now it feels the definition of selfish may be misunderstood.

"I am complete" – when I can write those words and mean them this journal will be finished before I am.

"Go There With Me"

Dec. 15

    Confusion, anger, sadness, hopelessness fills me again. One more day to teach before winter break. The parent who called complaining a week ago now wants her son moved to the other Kindergarten class. I see clearly how her son is manipulating her and how she is denying it. I know this behavior because I lived it. You and I did not dance this dance when you were five. It began for us in about the sixth grade. Although I know in my head that this is her and her son's lesson to learn, it frustrates me to be in the middle of it and not be heard. It is my hope she will learn it without too much pain or loss. The little boy is brighter then she gives him credit. At age five he already knows how to make her believe he has no idea his behavior is so disruptive to his classmates and he should not be held accountable.
    The total picture goes unseen – not meant to be viewed by those who are in the midst of participating. My lesson to learn. This young parent hears what she is ready to hear. She will learn by experiencing, not by my sharing what I see and know to be true.

Dec. 17

One of the perks of being numbed by your death was all the physical pain I usually felt had been ignored – not noticed for many months. I was so filled with the newness of grief I paid no attention to the nearly constant aching I have in my back and neck. Now, four months later, I encounter both the old familiar physical pain and my spiritual pain. Does this mean I am leaving the "numb" stage of grief? Ain't progress grand!

Dec. 18

Sadness is my constant companion. 'Tis the season I guess. I am so lonely inside. There is no reason to be with others. They do not reach that empty place that was you, Matt. I will be having breakfast with Jim tomorrow. I don't know why. I haven't seen much of him for over a month. The lack of grounding I receive from being with him is taking its toll. This would be a very easy time to leave. God, you brought Jim into my life and made it very clear for me why we are friends. Now it seems that is dying, too. What is the lesson? Show me. [When your mind is clear, listen. Your answers will be there.] I am tiring of "your answers are within, listen." Nothing is within except empty space! [Allow yourself to go into the emptiness – with guidance. It will help you. Do not go there with alcohol and pills – go there with me.]

Dec. 20

More closet "rearranging" in your room. I am unable to throw or give much away. I did find more of your writings. Notes written in preparation of a paper on your beliefs about God, for a psychology class you took at American River College. Also a completed paper titled "Christmas Day." Written at a time when you were experiencing a lot of anger from your dad's family. The notes of your thoughts about God were a Christmas present for me and a reminder of the wondrousness of you.

and then there was one

class notes:

Creating A Humanistic God
by Matt Williams

A person should have their own relationship with whatever kind of God they believe in.

God should not be used as a money making scheme. The God I believe in isn't short of cash.

People should not punish themselves in the name of their God so they can say, "Look how holy I am.."

People should be able to lead a good life without a promise of heaven and a threat of hell.

If you want to find your God, the best place to look is not in a church or bible. It's in your own heart.
God should be something simple and natural, not something full of rituals and mystery.

Your God should not be something you look up to and feel inferior to; it should be something you are a part of.

God to me is in myself, not something I have to wait until I'm dead to become a part of.

more notes:

Nirvana
by Matt Williams

You don't need to know where hurts come from to get rid of them.

The roads you travel on your way to inner peace are your choice.

Forgive your mom, for she knows not what she does.

Forgive all other non perfect human beings, so you can forgive yourself for your own transgressions.

and then there was one

Leaving for the Last Time

Dec. 21

When you left home to live in Ukiah I lost sight of my goal which has always been your well-being – as I perceived it "should" be. Your moving away was a "letting go" of the dependence I had around defining who I was as only your mom. I was beginning to look further into myself. Even enjoying the view. Especially enjoying being so proud of you, son, separate from me and overcoming all the adversities in your life. Is that what happened? You learned your lessons and were complete for this lifetime? If this is true then what of mine? What more could there be? What is my purpose now? Will my last lesson also be suicide?

Dec. 22

I am feeling very cranky. I wish all this Christmas "stuff" was over. I was telling this to my pastor, Steve, and he said it sounded reasonable to him and, "that

and then there was one

we all tend to lose sight of what was really happening at Christmas. We get entangled with what we think it is supposed to look like when it is really about Mary, a pregnant, unwed, homeless woman who had traveled more than a hundred miles by donkey, with the IRS after her, to give birth to our Lord in the home of some poor people." She was fortunate to have a man named Joseph who chose to be with her. You would have liked Steve, Matt. He has helped me many times make sense of the whys of what was happening to me. Mostly by suggesting I stop asking "why?."

Others have survived more tragic lives than yours, but you committed suicide. The drugs, always the drugs. Will they always win? Are my drinking and pill-taking revenge for your death? (*Talk to Steve and Gail and Marilyn, mom. Don't hide any more.*)

What is the matter with a God who kills you and lets horrible people live? (*God didn't kill me. We all did. It happened because it had to for the lessons you must all experience.*) The price is too high to pay. I want my son!

My mad raging scares our cat, Tiger and he disappears. This brings me back in control and I stop wailing and begin calling for Tiger to comfort him. The only living thing in my house to comfort. I was not there to comfort you my wounded and wailing son as you died – alone in a closet.

Dec. 23

I remember having two dreams last night, one more vivid than the other. They both involved looking for you. The first took place on our street and during

The Great Conspiracy of the Living

a huge Christmas party with the neighbors. I was looking everywhere and asking everyone for your whereabouts, but could not find you. I was not panicked, only very confused.

The only clear memory of the second dream was that it also involved a fruitless search. I awoke with the usual reality. You are no more.

Today I bought the only Christmas present I will be giving this year. It is for you. I arranged for a leather craftsman to make a soft leather pouch to hold your ashes. I need to keep them with me a while longer, and want you out of the cardboard box, son. How is it I can so calmly write about ordering a container for my child's ashes?

Everyone seems very worried that I do not want to join in on the Christmas doings – yet I know they understand why. I feel no need to celebrate this year and hold Christmas in my heart, not in decorations or presents. What is it like for Jesus this time of year? (*Confusing and amusing.*) Will you come to the candlelight service with me? (*I'll be there.*) How will I know? (*An angel will tell you.*) Good night, son. I love you and hold you in my heart wishing I was holding you in my arms.

Dec. 24 – a.m.

The sounds in the family room are often heard around 10:00 p.m. I have always believed them to be spirits of my mother and father. It was the room they spent the most time in when they lived here. I have heard the sounds since their deaths in 1977 and 1978. Today while I was sitting in the living room reading, the sounds began again. When I put my book down and turned toward the sounds, they ceased. I got my dowsing rods and went into the room. The rods remained closed, meaning no energy, until I was in the middle of the room and also near a corner by the window and then they opened wide. The sounds returned and I felt an overwhelming presence of all three of you. Tears fell and the sadness and loneliness from missing you overcame me. It is Christmas eve and although most of our Christmas eves with them were dysfunctional, they were ours together and I miss them. Were you truly here or was my imagination on overload? (*We're all here, mom, and even more than you know. We send our love and know you will survive this, too.*) You forgot something. I don't want to survive this one. (*Yes you do. You just don't know it yet.*)

Dec. 24 – p.m.

Tonight Aunt Sydnee gave me an angel and at church there was an angel on the Christmas tree that I had not seen before. Steve did not stick with the program as written and as the service ended had us sing "Hark the Herald Angels Sing." All the angels were telling me of your presence. I wore your blue and black sweater and felt you with me. Tomorrow I am going to brunch with Jim. I am not sure why.

Dec. 25

My first Christmas without you has passed. Barb was right. The anticipation prior to the actual event is the worst part. I kept very busy with friends today and did not feel you here at all. I am getting a sense that you left last night when I returned from the candlelight service at church and had two drinks before going to sleep. There is a terrible battle going on inside me. I know I am supposed to stay, my left brain talking, but I want so much not to be in this emptiness anymore, my right brain. I am not drinking tonight, son. Come into my dream time and be with me there.

Dec. 28

Listening for sounds of your truck and then your confident footsteps coming up the walk was really the beginning of Christmas for me. Not the tree and decorations or cookies I have baked for you since you were a baby. I did not know the sounds would still be expected – still listened for. My brain understands you will not be home this holiday; however, my heart and soul have not communicated with it since last July.

I did okay the first week of vacation. Secure in knowing I was not "doing Christmas" this year and that was all right. But as the time grew closer to when you would have been coming home to visit, my sadness began to overtake all other feelings and the panic attacks returned. I have stayed away from the department stores and even the grocery store, going out to dinner with friends or eating fast food from the drive-ins. Today at the drugstore I saw Valentine items on the shelves. And so it goes on – life. Another "why?" comes to mind.

Dec. 29

In the middle of the night Tiger made his usual trek from his blanket at the foot of my bed to right up by my neck, purring full blast. He lay there with my arms around him for quite awhile – our middle-of-the-night ritual. I was just falling asleep when suddenly he sat up, and sitting very still, looked in the direction of the headboard and wall and for about three minutes just sat there in the dark, staring, not moving a bit. Then he turned and went to his blanket where he lay down and fell asleep.

Dec. 31

It is about 6:15 a.m. and I have been awake thinking of you and was reminded that there is some amount of shame attached to your suicide. The "if I did more – if I had been more aware of my son's needs – if I had been a better mother, Matt would not be dead" stuff weighs heavy today. All these accusations and more pierce my heart. *(It was not about you. You were the best. Always there for me.)* What happened then, Matt? What went wrong? Will I ever know these answers? *(Maybe not so you can understand now. Maybe you just need to accept that it happened and you could not have done anything more or differently. You have no need for shame. You were the mom I chose. The mom I needed to have for this lifetime. I love you for all you did for me. Please don't be so sad. The shame is not yours. It belongs to all who participated in the death that is still taking place every day around the drugs and the judgmental attitudes and lack of caring that lead young people to look for escape. Perhaps my death is proof it can happen to anybody's son.)*

Jan. 1, 1995

Jim came for dinner last night. There is a change not talked about, yet still the familiar and comfortable friendship remains.

Jan. 3

Every time I tell someone new of your death you die all over again and I have to struggle to stay alive. The decision to live or die is still an everyday choice for me. Right now living is a habit, not a commitment. Choosing to stay frightens me more than dying, son. *(I know mom. You are being guided toward the decision for a reason.)*

and then there was one

Where is the Rule Book?

Jan. 4

There were three of you Matt. This is what you told me in a dream months ago. Now I understand. One was the rebel; challenging life and craving excitement. Another was a strong, loving person, giving to all in need of reassurance of their worth, because he had a sureness about himself and what he stood for. The third asked silent questions of everyone he met. Am I enough? Am I doing it right – this life thing? It feels like I'm not. It feels like I am going to disappear. Notice me. See me.

You were enough Matt. And now you are gone.

Jan. 6

A half year since you died, Matt. Time is surreal. Sometimes the days and nights seem to take forever to get through, yet the months rush by.

The beginning of a new year had a strange effect on my mood. I became more out of touch with my "grief" and was living and reacting as I did before your death. I had to remind myself what my reality is. "Don't you remember? Your son shot himself. He will not be here anymore. No more calls, no more problems to solve together. No "future." It was my first glimpse of the possibility of a future without you.

While driving home from a movie I remember thinking – why did they make that picture and why did I go to it? I am being caught up in a great conspiracy of those who go on living even though you are not alive. If I were dead people would still make movies and people would still go to see them. Does life have any meaning past your memorial service? You are missed and many important things will not happen because you died, but no one really talks about you anymore. The only time I hear your name is if I say it. It is as if you were never here. YOU WERE HERE. I have a need to talk about you. To keep you real.

The pitcher of tea is still in the refrigerator.

Jan. 8

Why am I the only one who is keeping track of how long you have been dead? I was the one who kept track of your years alive, gave the birthday parties, bought presents, celebrated. What do I do about these milestones? Where is the rule book to tell me the protocol for the death of a son?

Jan. 11

A letter to God:
I miss you God, and I want you back in my life, but I am so angry that you took my son – my life. I feel so left alone. Devastated by the emptiness. Why did you use Matt for this lesson in my life? What am I supposed to do? Surrendering what is left of me to you, feels like the ultimate test of trust. Show me what you want. Allow me to be open and see what I am to do. My wanting to die and be with Matt is keeping me stuck. I need to know why he killed himself. I need to forgive myself for not being enough reason for him to live. Self-forgiveness is so difficult. If I surrender my life to you, I have to forgive myself. Why is my life more important than his was? Why is he dead and not me?

Jan. 12

When did waking with the knowledge of your death begin to feel normal? Is it the beginning of healing or just the beginning of existing without you? (*Your choice mom.*) Happy birthday to me.

Jan. 19

I looked up the word normal in the Thesaurus and found forty synonyms – none of which is appropriate for what I am feeling. It defies description. The closest I can come is to say I have become a "human doing," and am no longer a "human being," keeping very busy so I have no time to ponder my life.

Jan. 20

It is said we never step into the same river twice because the water is constantly flowing. The sound of the river must also be the slightest bit different at any given moment in time. When we cry, we never cry the same tears. Each one is new, bringing relief from the damn built by the survivor's attempt to "hold up" under impossible circumstances. For me, tears that come to clear the soul and repair the heart, cloud my vision with sorrow that restricts their flow, diminishing the clarity I need to find my way through this. It is my prayer that the time will come when what keeps me going is not my assurance that death is still a choice for me, but that it isn't even an option. In truth, I find myself between the two. Preparing my house, possessions, will, etc., in readiness for my planned death in July, and going on with my life, taking new classes, traveling, buying new things, in other words, making plans for a future.

Jan. 22

I find going to church very difficult. Epecially if I have been going through the week on autopilot, numb, just doing what needs doing. The people there are so genuine and clear about their love that I cannot get away with "not feeling" when I am in their presence. At my church there is no need for pretense. Everyone gets to be who they are and feel what they are feeling, even if it is uncomfortable for a while. I do not tell them enough how much it means to me that this caring community of human beings exists.

Jan. 26

I still plug in your answering machine once in a while so I can hear your voice. "Letting go" of your life remains so difficult. It seems lately I have been pretending you are still alive. It is easy to do because I did not see you very often this past year, and I want so much for it to be true. Then something will happen and reality hits me square in the heart once again.

January, and a new school semester. You had talked of transferring to Humboldt State in January. More future plans unfulfilled. Another confirmation that you are no more. I read that recovery from grief is possible once unrealistic hopes for a lost future are given up. I have given up on your future – and my own. I do not think that is what the writer meant.

Jan. 27

I no longer feel attachment or commitment to this life and look with a curiosity at people, wondering why they go on with their lives and expect me to do the same. As if it were an important thing to do.

Jan. 31

I receive comfort in the belief that where you are now there is love all around you and you are accepting it – knowing you deserve it. Unlike here where you were never sure. You always measured your worth through the eyes of others. A great lesson we can receive from you now is how futile that was. Toward the end of your life you talked and wrote of self worth, yet did not hear your own words – or believe they could be true for you. I know they are true for you now. My soul aches for that truth, too.

The Science Fiction Movie People

Feb. 2

Aunt Sydnee and I went to a bereavement group tonight. There was a lecture on "The need to grieve." The speaker talked about the "stages" again. The people there are akin to people in a science fiction movie, dropped off on a planet and placed all together in a room. They have some things in common, but each is alone in the bewilderment that brought them there. Each trying to make sense of why they are in this circumstance.

Everything remains surreal to me. Things happen at work – rooms damaged and vandalized, buses not on time, schedules not met. These become crises to those involved. Don't they know these are only inconveniences? They can be repaired. You, my son, are dead. You are a box of ashes, irreparable. I do not mean to judge what is important and what is not. I am living in a different dimension, trying to find my way back. No map is available so far.

Feb. 5

It is only February 5th, yet Spring seems to be here. The trees and flowers blossom and everything is coming back to life. Everything except you Matt, and me. I still do not want to be alive without you. In a few months it will be your birthday. Now you have a birthday and a "deathday." This is too much. It is as if in your dying a part of me was removed and my life's blood is draining away through the unhealed wound.

It is Sunday night. I dread Sunday nights, knowing tomorrow I must go to work and once again somehow pull it together and pretend I am not going crazy. Not consumed with missing you. Not consumed with the thought of you, lying in a dark closet for three days, dead and bleeding – alone.

Feb. 6

Sleep does not come easily and once I am asleep, I no longer dream. My sleep is so deep that when I wake up my body feels like it weighs six hundred pounds, pleading with me not to get up, to just let it lie there in bed where I do not have to think or do anything. I am just hanging on until vacation time, tiring of being two different people. The one I let others see and the true me. The person who is disappearing and losing her grasp of what is real.

Feb. 9

I have been ignoring you and your death. Pretending again, floating, detached. Outside of my body most of the time, observing. Seeing me at work, at home, with friends – not present. Spring brings life to this world I no longer want to be a part of. The guilt of this weighs heavily on me. I know there are many people who are dying and want to live. I would change places with them, give them my life if I could, so I could be with you, son.

and then there was one

Unwanted Life Support

Feb. 11

I have sold your truck to Paul. I know you want Nathan to have it. The two of you spent a lot of time and energy on it. It is something tangible Nate has left that was a part of you, something he can use in his journey through his grief. A bridge from having you with him, to finally letting go when he is ready to sell it. It is also a final "letting go" of any remaining connection I have with your dad. This feels complete.

Feb. 16

Although I haven't felt your presence with me lately, you continue to communicate with me, son, through memories, new found papers you wrote while in college, and an old letter I had forgotten about. This connection always seems to come when I am searching for an answer or when I need comfort or reassurance that, yes you really did once live – you were here and you made a difference. I will be sharing with my friends part of the letter you wrote to me before you left home to be on your own for the last time. You were a young man of insight and have something to say that they may need to hear as they process detaching from their children or parts of themselves that no longer serve them. Each time I read the letter I receive more understanding of you and me and us, at times seeing very clearly what I "should" have done that might have changed the outcome of your life. Other times feeling very guilty for not interfering – not being more aware of your pain, yet knowing interfering would have been disrespectful of you and would not really have changed anything in the end.

Feb. 18

I am slowly drowning in tears of the loss from your death; never to hear your voice, touch your cheek, feel your joy or pain – life extinguished. The cruelty of having to be alive without you in my life remains unbearable. I feel like I am on a life-support system without the tubes and machine. My family and friends are that system, and somehow I gave them permission to hook me up to it. It is very difficult to release from them. Necessary though if I am to go on from this life and be with you, son.

Feb. 20

Since your death I have prayed for an illness that would take my life. I know it sounds selfish and crazy, yet I believe we can keep ourselves healthy or cause disease. If I am able to do this, it will be the first time my body has done what I want it to do. There have been so many times when it has betrayed me with illnesses I did not want, maybe this time it will comply. With my death I can be with you and God. This sounds very welcoming, I am so tired of being. Death does not frighten me. My spirituality has grown these past two years and I have a great calmness and certainty about an afterlife. I need to get busy and finish things here in the house and at school so I will be ready. I know this must sound so morbid to some who will read it, yet it is truly the opposite.

Feb. 22

What do I do with all the keepsakes left from your life? The toys carefully saved for grandchildren that are not to be, record albums and books collected through the years? And when I am gone what will become of our pictures and your things that are important only to me? I want my family to know they need only keep what they want and to share the rest of our things with anyone who wants them. I will have made one photo album of our life together. There is no need to "hold on to" any more pictures. You and I will live in their memories and that is enough. God is my strength and has enabled me to continue without you so far, but it is taking everything out of me to get through the week. I end up sleeping most of the weekend away, when I have so much to do.

and then there was one

❧ Dead. Not Lost!

Feb. 23

Everything I do feels like a lie. I went to the Bereavement Group again tonight and took my friend Jean — her husband died last year. There are too many people there, too much pain, too much talk about healing from the "loss." You are not LOST! You are DEAD. Why do they all say "I lost my mother, husband, son, etc."? If you were lost, there would be a possibility of finding you, and then myself. We are gone. I just haven't left my body completely yet.

Feb. 24

There are ways to experience the death of a child other than physical death. For some it comes with a grave illness or accident that renders the child different than before. For others this change is apparent when all you believe is good, and right for your child is not coming to fruition. The future you worked and planned for is suddenly not shared by your child anymore. Thoughts of this came to me after listening to a friend talk of her son's present journey through life. The surprise comes with not knowing from the beginning that we parents have very little influence or control over what happens in this change from adolescence to adulthood. We often find it difficult to accept this rebellion of our beliefs after investing so many years with this cherished part of us – our child. The truth comes in understanding that they come into this life with their own agendas, not clean slates for us to write a future on. Gibran said it best when he wrote, "our children come through us but not from us." And the separation when the umbilical cord is severed or the adoption paper signed is the beginning of the letting go – birth. A spiritual cord remains, allowing us to be their guides through this life. But it often becomes entangled with our own to the point of strangulation for both parent and child, especially at the times when we need a clear and thinking brain the most. It is painful to watch as our child does self-destructive behavior in this journey to untangle the cord. It tears at the heart and is especially difficult if our own cords were never smoothly severed from our parents. We are all left dangling, not really connected and yet not strong enough to break away cleanly and continue our journey, separate and whole, free to experience life, accepting and owning both the joy and the pain. I held on too long, firmly attached to your cord, Matt. Not seeing where mine ended and yours began, it was not until the last year of your life that we began celebrating this "letting go." But you were not fully prepared and needed something else to rely on – the drugs. I am reminded of part of a poem you wrote – "Drugs are a trip, but they always take you home."

Were you talking about the safe feeling you had when we were attached? (*That's part of it, mom. I knew you would always be there for me, but a man needs to let go, even if he fucks it up. Otherwise he needs something else or someone else besides himself to make him feel enough.*) **If I had let you "fuck up" and feel the consequences when you were younger, you would have had the confidence to get through the really difficult stuff as you got older.** (*Let it go, mom, you did what you were supposed to. So did I. You are still holding on too tight.*) **The lesson continues.**

and then there was one

KNOWLEDGE
by Matt Williams

Drugs are a trip,
but they always take you home.
Why spend life sitting on a couch
with a joint in your hand,
waiting for something to happen?
I want to make things happen.
Working all day at a job I hate -
what a waste.
Only to fuck the same girl, or sit
at the same cafe and drink coffee from
the same cup while life slips by.
Knowledge is what I need.
It's the only real high.
The only real escape from a life of
boredom and father time.

My Guiding Angel

Feb. 26

While listening to Steve's sermon in church today I heard him talk of a miracle that had occurred in Jesus' time that gave a man back his son. I silently asked myself, "When will God give Matt back to me?" and in my thoughts God answered – [Look and listen for the truth. When you know it, you will have your son back and your soul will be with you again.] It was then I knew that perhaps I am supposed to stay in this life and not pray for my death or cause it. This brings me deeper into the "anger stage" of grief.

Feb. 27

I was right about the anger. It fills me with fear. The possibility of living this life without you, my son, has not been my plan. Now that the choice has been taken, I am left more confused than ever. I will need to listen to the tape of Steve's sermon, because I do not understand what God was telling me.

March 2

This is an impossible place to be – driven and exhausted by the anger of not wanting to believe what I know is beginning to be my truth. I am supposed to "go on with life," "not give up," and whatever other stupid cliche there is about surviving. I borrowed the tape from Steve and will listen to him again and try to make sense out of my new and unwelcome "revelation."

After listening, I find I am angry, furious with Steve. Sermons are expected to be general interpretations of passages from the bible, telling us what we "should be," or "should do," reminding us of our transgressions. But Steve's are not at all like that. With his words he always manages somehow, to reach each of us with a message that feels as if it were ment only for that person. He spoke of God's miracle and I began questioning. Until then I had a plan, a way to end this pain, a way out. *(You know he is making sense, mom. Listen some more.)*

March 3

What I am coming to understand is that truth is the awesome power and strength inside me. Truth is the miracle that a mother could survive her child and that faith and prayer – whatever that is for each of us – is more powerful than the need to self-destruct. The power of God is trustable. When I allow healing to occur, I will no longer feel separate from you, Matt. You will truly be with me and I can go on and continue my life journey. The "road map" is inside my trust and faith. I pray the directions will be clear to me and I will be open to understand them, and then perhaps be able to help clear the path for others who are also "map illiterate." This power is beyond ourselves and yet lives in us waiting to be discovered and used when needed. We are all given to each other for whatever time. The going on without you is not the miracle for me. It is the coming to the place where I want to go on. I will need lots of help, son. Send all the angels and guides you can. Maybe someday you will be one of my guides. *(I am one already, mom. I always have been.)* Yes, Matthew - gift of God. You continue to be my best gift. And with new knowledge I understand even the most difficult lessons we learned together were gifts and important paths we followed in our life together. For today, son, I am back and will continue for you, with you and because of you.

and then there was one

PART THREE

Searching

and then there was one

The Carmel River Woman

March 7

Eight months without you. I have been feeling a new peace that has not been a part of me since you died, yet the loneliness of a childless mother remains. There is a sadness no one can touch, not even God at this time. Only memories of you can share this cave I retreat into at this time each month. In this "cave" I am with you in your closet – will I ever lose that vision? (*I'm sorry, mom. Don't remember me there. See me at the computer writing or driving my truck or at home with you. Remember me alive.*)

March 10

The "going on" phase was very uplifting for about five days. It is good to know I can touch that feeling inside me again; however, there is a great amount of sadness connected to the "going on" without you. I leave today for a weekend at Asilomar – refuge by the sea.

March 11

The sun is shining after weeks of grey sky and rain. I prefer the greyness. It seems more appropriate. The drive here was very stormy and there was some flooding on the road. Four other teachers and I have traveled to Asilomar to a Reading Conference. I do not plan to attend many sessions. The getting away with friends is my goal and is intended to be part of my healing. I joke and laugh with my friends and pretend to forget the pain for a while.

Presently I am sitting on the beach, thinking of you and feeling you sitting next to me, imagining your arm around my shoulders. Knowing I am only touching and hearing you in my mind is a very lonely thing. The world and I move on without you, but the rhythm of that moving is missing a beat – you. As each of us die, no matter the circumstance, the rhythm is altered and it takes time and perhaps new "music lessons" to get back in step. Or maybe a new dance needs to be choreographed. Doing my life dance without you, Matt – well, I never was very musical!

March 12

We are stuck on the Monterey Peninsula. The Carmel river flooded and the highway is covered with water. All are feeling the need to leave for various reasons and the strain of forced levity is beginning to show. A room is rented in Carmel and we will stay the night. Hopefully the road will be passable by morning. Five women living together in one small room no matter where, or how good the friendships,

Searching

is a whole new lesson in tolerance.

Tonight I was feeling very claustrophobic and a panic attack was beginning. I went out walking to retrieve the feeling of my own space and to calm myself. While walking I passed by a woman I had noticed the day before while shopping. She lives in an enclosed bus stop next to a park. She simply sits on the bench all wrapped up in clothes and blankets with a hat pulled down around her face. Questions come to mind. When does she eat, what brought her here, can she walk, is she an angel? I know that last one sounds absurd, yet when I looked at her and made eye contact, her face was so beautiful and serene looking. She appears to be a very large woman, but that may be all the clothes and blankets. People respond to her presence as if she were invisible. Yet it is the noticing that is important. I felt a connection to her, wrapped in her cocoon as I am wrapped in mine. There was some amount of envy in what I experienced – knowing how safe I feel wrapped up surrounded only by me and not letting the rest of the world in. When we looked into each other's souls, I knew it was what kept her there, too. It is comforting to know that place of safety is always available to visit, but unlike her, I no longer want to remain there. (*You don't belong there, mom – don't give up, too. You saw some of me in her and that is why you kept returning to her. She and I simply chose a different exit.*) Will I ever understand your need to "exit"? (*I hope not.*)

and then there was one

"Keep a Stout Heart!"

March 15

    You were about three years old, snuggled in my arms as we sat on a grassy hillside. I was peacefully rocking you and very aware we were in my dream, yet able to feel the comfort of your little warm body as we sat in the sun. It was the same when you were alive. The energy you created and gave to others with such empathy and understanding always amazed me. We rocked for a long time before I felt the arm of my grown-up son securely around my shoulder as the little "you" faded away.

    As we sat on the hill together in the dream, it felt as if a mistake had been made and you were really still alive. We sat and talked for a long time and I wanted the dream to go on forever. It was so real. Being asleep is my place of preference these days. I did not awake with a clearness of what we talked about, and am hoping to remember more of this dream. (*It means I have not completely left you, mom. As long as there is you, there will be me.*) But not out here, Matt. Not where I have to be most of the time. (*I am there as much as I can be. You need to find your way there, without me.)* This new beginning is not working for me. You have been part of me for almost half of my life. It is as if a part of me has been amputated and I still have the phantom pains and feelings.

March 17

I was so good at hanging onto my anger most of the time. You were the only one I felt safe enough to express it to. That part of our relationship holds many regrets for me. It made you older than your years and gave you an unrealistic view of how to express anger. In looking farther back to the time when grandma and grandpa cared for you while I was in college and after I began teaching, I realize all their love for you did not balance out the environment created by the two sad and depressed people they had become. Why do I revisit these old places in my memory? (*They are part of the unsolvable puzzle you're attempting to put together to answer the "why" questions about me, mom.*) All the experiences I created for you, and the ones you created with the information you received and interpreted, formed your life on earth. Accepting that each lesson connected to the ultimate ending of your life, is a difficult thing indeed for a mother to live with. It is no different from leaving a toddler alone for only minutes who then ends up drowning in a swimming pool. Neither episode was expected nor intended. Time is irrelevant – twenty-three years preceeding a child's death or four minutes. The outcome remains and remains and remains.

Searching

March 18

"Keep a stout heart!" Gentle words told to me by a new neighbor as I return home from my visit with her. Her husband of forty-five years died two years ago this month. Another connection.

March 19

A wind storm felled a tree in our back yard and it clung to the phone and electrical wires, holding on until I returned from Asilomar. The discovery was made just before my departure, but I ignored it, considering it an inconvenience, not a problem needing immediate attention. Upon returning on Monday, I called the appropriate offices and arranged for the tree and wires to be taken care of. The electric company cut the tree loose and left a huge mess in the yard. One of our neighbors agreed to cut the large limbs and take the wood for his fireplace. I told him I would take care of the rest. The smaller branches covered the yard and I managed to put off doing anything about them until today at about four o'clock. It was while cutting and hauling that the anger I have been ignoring began to surface. Then the tears, and with the tears, the rain. With every muscle and joint in by body hurting, I kept cutting and hauling, knowing the physical pain did not even come close to the emotional pain. I was angry with you for not being here to help me – realistically knowing you would not have been here anyway. You lived in Ukiah. But at least I could have called and complained to you about it. The anger is also centered around a friend I love and care about. She has been very occupied with her son, but still makes plans with me, then breaks them with little thought of my feelings. It happened again today. Plans made, only to be changed for the convenience of her son. The anger exists around the fact that she has a son and I no longer do. If you had had the opportunities, this young man has been lucky enough to have been given, I believe you would still be alive. *(It is his life mom, not mine.)* I am aware none of this makes sense Matt, and I am still allowed to feel angry! *(And that makes a lot of sense.)*

March 25

Dear God, center of my being. Thank you for the recognition that you have returned to me – that you never left me.

Burt's Shirts

March 26

    Yesterday was a sunny and windy and "it's time to go shopping" kind of day. I went to midtown and ended up in a little garden shop where I bought a teeshirt with grandpa's name on it – a picture of corn and the words "Burt's Shirts" on the side of the picture. An image came to me of when you were four and announced you "wanted to be a farmer like grandpa and grow corn and big beautiful snails." I bought the shirt to wear as I plant a garden in our yard where you and grandpa planted one together so long ago. With purchase complete, I was on my way down the street when the toe of my shoe caught part of the broken sidewalk. I completely lost my footing and landed on the right side of my forehead! Shoulder, arm, and ribs got the next blow. Mind separate from body, I watched myself sit up and examine my head. It seemed all I could do was just sit there. What I wanted to do was get to my car, yet aware I was not able to drive. The whole incident was very embarrassing. An angel in the disguise of a young man came over to attend to me. By now I had quite a large bump on my head. He called for someone from the garden store to take me inside while he went for ice. I remember going in and sitting down. They were all very kind. I was having great difficulty remembering phone numbers and who my medical insurer was. I finally formulated your aunt's phone number in my brain and the clerk dialed it for me. Sydnee said she would send Lisa over to get me right away. I was continuing to have difficulty processing information and must have asked the clerk his shop address three times before I could tell Aunt Syd. I sat with ice on my head and waited as my eyes became very unfocused. I now know what people mean when they talk of "seeing stars" after a blow to the head. Lisa and Jamie arrived and took me to the clinic where I was x-rayed and judged to have a concussion, but no broken bones.

As I awoke this morning, I asked myself what I learned from this experience. **1.** I am definitely not going to finish clearing the limbs in the yard myself. Everything hurts today! **2.** I have strong bones and a hard head. (*Known fact, mom!*) Very amusing. **3.** It is easier to allow people to help me and to be taken care of than it used to be. (*Then why didn't you stay overnight at Aunt Syd's like the doctor said to?*) I said easier, not easy. **4.** We all deserve to be helpers and to be helped. I wish I had modeled that one for you more often.

Searching

March 27

What comes to mind today, exhausted after teaching and "keeping up with" thirty-one kindergartners, is that perhaps I am experiencing this physical pain to somehow explain or show the emotional pain I have been living with. People can see this. My eye is black and blue, my head tender, and every part of me aches. "You see I really am hurting – this is the way it looks inside too, only one hundred times worse." I don't think anyone got it.

and then there was one

Life Renewing - Another <u>Why?</u> Question

March 29

Today I attended a training session for a new program to be implemented at my school. It is called Student Assistance Program. When the principal asked for volunteers and I heard myself saying I would be interested it was as though someone else had agreed. (*It was me influencing you, mom.*) That explains it. The training would not be for months and I managed to put it out of my mind until today. We were given the materials and as we began talking and reading, the reality of what this training was about hit me. There I was, being confronted first with painful memories of my own childhood with alcoholic parents, and next with the reminder of being a mother who lived through most of her son's adolescence in denial of his drug abuse and depression. The presenters said many things that were difficult for me to hear, but it is giving me another link in understanding you and what you did. I feel you are there in the room with many others who have also died because of the lack of comprehension, or the need to deny by those close to them. (*That's part of the whole picture.*)

March 30

Matt, why is this information coming to me now? Where was it when you were alive and why didn't I get you help? (*You wanted me to be okay, mom. You wanted to believe in me. I wasn't honest with you. You aren't remembering what I was really like as a teenager – stop glorifying me. I know you will always feel you could have done more – maybe now is your chance. Just not on your terms.*) Be here and guide me.

April 3

I have put you away, Matt. My life just goes on and on and you are nowhere to be found. (*I am in your writing, mom.*) I do not feel you. Nine months this week. Have I given birth to the end of you? If so, I have given birth to the end of me. Spring break next week. My plans continue, with some changes. I will tie up loose ends during break.

April 7

I lie in a hot bath listening to music and as I do, tears come. These feel like the "getting ready" tears. (*You have decisions to make. You are beginning to mourn your own passing, knowing you will be leaving those you love, and have grown to care for and who rely on you.*)

Can't I do my work from the spiritual realm? *(Not in the same way.)* Who am I talking to? (It's me, mom, with others who are our teachers.) I want to be with you. This is lonely work, this life stuff. I am weary of staying. *(Use your week off to rest and listen and write. Mostly rest.)* But what about my plans to get things in order? *(Just do the taxes and whatever brings you peace. You fell and hurt your body to force yourself to rest. You never listen to it. The pain won't go if you fight it.)* Talk to me of my school and everything that is happening there. *(Not now – let it go.)*

April 8

Help me to understand what is happening at work. Explain the conflicts and my part in them. I did not want to be "involved" in school politics this year, but have landed right in the middle of some very difficult and painful stuff. *(Your principal needs to surround herself with those who are not in touch with their spiritual sides. Those who are, frighten her. She feels something missing in herself and is not willing, at this time, to delve deep enough within to find it. Her spiritual void. Some other staff members are in the same place and safe for her to be with. Connie is between the two – seeing both and deciding it is time to make her own life choice. She sees some of herself in them. This is how she recognizes them for who they are and what their journey is. She also sees beyond, with new wisdom. She knows where they are. It is not enough for her anymore.)* Should I tell Connie this or let her get it for herself? *(She is getting it. We are guiding you in this work.)* Then I have to stay alive longer? *(You know that answer is only yours.*) There are many confused and discouraged people on the staff. It is my sense their questions will not be answered and their concerns will not be heard at this time. Some will choose to transfer to other schools. More loss.

April 11

Jim took me to breakfast this morning. Once again he has asked the questions I needed to hear to help put a problem in perspective. I had described the concerns at work and the feelings of betrayal among many of the staff. I told him of our plan to inform the principal of our grievances in the hope she would hear us and want to work at uniting the staff rather then pulling it apart. He said she must be in a lot of pain and fear to create what is taking place. I think this causes her to behave ineffectively and with very narrow vision.

Later in the day I worked on your taxes, Matt. Doing this brought me back to last July. Tears, confusion, loss. This is one more truth that proves there is no longer Matthew Warren Williams, alive and contributing to this planet. Tomorrow is Wednesday. I rested most of Monday. Went crazy Tuesday. I am feeling very disconnected and weepy. The need to have you alive and the pain of knowing, really knowing you will never be again does not diminish. I am so scared tonight. (*The safety is in our writing.*)

April 12

I had a dream about you last night. You were about six or seven and were outside choosing a tree for a rope swing, like the one you used to have. There did not seem to be a tree in our yard and you were looking in the neighbors' yards. The dream ended before we found just the right tree. (*I never felt rooted to this life, mom.*)

April 16

We celebrated our first Easter without you, Matt. As I watched the little ones hunt for eggs and gobble up as much candy as they could get away with, my thoughts returned to you at their age. You were quieter, more serious and every bit as precious.

Last year you came home to visit and I cooked for you. Inge, Darrell and Jim joined us. You were supposed to join us and be here today, Matt. (*No mom, I'm where I'm supposed to be.*)

Spring has been especially difficult this year. Life renewing itself. I receive spurts of clear thinking, seeing me living without you. Then it goes away. (*Look closer and don't feel guilty about it.*)

I, too, have been going through a process of renewal without even knowing it. Something I used to take for granted was that you would always be in my life. What comes to me more and more is that my choice of living here without you or not living is being taken away. Time passes. I keep busy. I go numb and stop feeling the pain of your death and I sometimes see through the pain to my life that is still here

and then there was one

and to all the people I love and would hurt by dying as you did. (*Remember it does not have to be your choice to leave, mom. You were the mom I chose, now find out what else you are chosen for.*)

Will I ever stop crying when I think of you? (*No, you will probably always need to do some of that.*)

Mother's Day No Longer

April 18

 Jason J. called me today, speaking as if I would welcome his call. He said he recently heard of your death, was very upset, and wanted to come and see me. He also said he was in a twelve-step program and asked me to forgive him for the trouble he caused a few years ago. I told him forgiving was not a problem, but that I did not trust him and asked him to call back in a few months when he had been on his program longer. He can ask for my forgiveness, yet if he is dependant on my doing it, he does not "get" the program. Asking unconditionally and without expectations is what it is about. I feel no need to see him and was very upset by his call. (*Not wanting to talk to Jason, is continuing to not face your denial of the drugs Jason and I did when we were younger.*) It feels like that time of your life was the beginning of the end of you. Yes, he reminds me of what I ignored, and therefore condoned, when the two of you were friends. He is surviving the youth you shared and he was much more outwardly affected by it than you, Matt. He said hearing about your death was instrumental in beginning recovery. (*I'm glad for him – we once had a strong connection that we both needed at the time. I also needed to disconnect and learn a painful lesson about that.*)

April 30

I have not been writing again. It seems all I have the energy to do is work, come home and go to sleep. I am feeling separated again; "acting out" the parts of many different people. Somehow this gives me the illusion of sanity. I no longer share my grief. This makes me once again "not real." I am very good at acting like everything is "just fine," when inside I am turning to embers as the life force is being extinguished. The person I show is who I am comfortable being with my loved ones and friends. I do not want to share my dying.

May 4

Although I feel you with me, I do not listen for you. I want to be with you, but know it is not time. This realization leaves me so angry and confused. I regret checking out on my friends and family, but will not share this desperation with them. I do not want to be here without you, Matt. (*You aren't, mom. I'm with you more now than when I was alive.*) It does not stop my sadness. It does not give me a future. I am alone without you, son. I want to be your mom. Who am I now – just someone who feels empty and sorry for herself? I do not like this me.

Searching

Mother's Day will be here soon. (*I was never too good at remembering things like that, but could always count on your reminders!*) The connection we have happened before birth and continues beyond death. I am realizing that I have Paul to thank, for he unknowingly was instrumental in this. His leaving us before you were born, not being a part of "us" allowed our relationship to develop as it has.

May 7

I have too many connections. The "letting go" will not be easy. How do I make the break with this life and leave these connections behind? Having the choice makes living without you possible for now. (*You have much more to do, mom. Much more to experience even without me.*) I want you in my dreams tonight, Matt. You were there ten months ago when you killed yourself. I ignored the dream. Come tonight and help me understand more clearly.

May 8

Dreams are rarely remembered longer than a few seconds upon wakening. I do not recall last night's dream, but have some clarity about my choice to live or not. It has to be about me wanting to be alive – not about living because of guilt. Jim is in my life because he simply loves and accepts my friendship, wanting no attachments that accompany an "in love" relationship. This is what I need now. My family and friends love me and feel helpless with my pain. How do I help them to know I understand their frustration, and that it may still not make the difference?

May 9

I am worried about my sister and nieces and how this will affect them. Syd will be taken care of. All I have will be hers. (*But she won't have a sister any more.*) I am not much of a sister to her now. If she would allow her daughters inside, to know her feelings, she would be complete with them. But she is too frightened to be there herself for very long. Don't worry about tomorrow, Syd. God is already there. Open yourself to today. You have so much waiting for you, so many wanting to know you. (*Listen to your own words.*) I know. But I want to be in spirit, Matt. I am too tired to reinvent me.
  I have three months left and lots to do. June will be the busiest time with the house and my "things." July will be busy with my writing and saying good by.
  I do not want to be alive without you, Matt.

May 13

I do not know what to write anymore. Tomorrow is Mother's Day – I am no longer a mother. (*I'm here, mom. As long as you know that, you know you are still my mom. I need you, mom, as much as ever. This writing keeps me alive. I am in between. Not ready to be dead and not alive.*) When I allow myself to feel you with me and to think about you I cannot do my day-to-day stuff – job, being with people, etc. the sadness overwhelms me, so I put you out of my thoughts. This leaves me detached, confused and it also causes me to forget things and not be fully alive. I, too, feel trapped between life and death. Having to live because my body is alive and wanting to be with you because my spirit is mostly not present in this body. I just want to be with you, son. I know you are with me, but I want to be with you.

May 14 Mother's Day

a.m.

This morning I woke up at 9:00, read the paper and stayed in bed watching movies all day. I pretty much avoided the whole Mother's Day.
Last night I dreamed you were home with me. While looking out of our window we saw a small plane slowly crashing into the neighbors' yards across the street. We went over to see if anyone was hurt and no one was. I guess it was about me. My life is still crashing down around me as I try not to let anyone get hurt in the fallout. I am glad you are near if I do crash.

p.m.

I went over to visit Jim this evening. He is my dear friend and temporary escape.
Now home, I return to the reality I do not want to face. I do not get to be the mother of a living child anymore.
The gift of life once given cannot be manipulated

and then there was one

by the giver.
    You killed yourself, not because you wanted to die, but to escape the pain of the moment, unable to see farther than the despair that was engulfing you. I miss you. I wish I could change what happened to you. I wish I had paid attention to my feelings when I talked to you the morning of your death. You sounded so distant. I assumed you were just tired, but it was more than that and this is what remains the mystery.

This Poor Excuse For An Airplane

May 18

I leave tomorrow on a trip to Sedona, Arizona and the Grand Canyon. I will be there on your birthday. Something is drawing me there. I am both frightened and anxious. I do not travel well and have yet to make accommodations. However my airplane ticket is purchased and the car rented. Will you come with me, Matt? (*Yes.*)

The leather pouch I ordered last Christmas was never made and I plan to have one crafted in Sedona.

May 19

And so my journey begins. I sit in the Phoenix airport waiting to fly to Flagstaff where I will rent a car and drive to Sedona. My eyes fill with tears and my throat tightens as I try not to cry. This journey is a mystery. I cannot be home and live through your

and then there was one

birthday without you and without answers I seek. (*You wonder what questions to ask.*) I have some ideas.

It is good to be on the trip alone. Although when first planned, I asked some friends if they would accompany me. None could get away at this time. And so it is, you and me on another vacation together. Last year at this time we were planning our trip to Ft. Bragg. I will always be grateful for that trip with you. (*We had fun and enjoyed most of it!*) One month later you took our life together away with one pull of the trigger. The questions emerge.

My trip resembles my thought processes of late. I assumed things were arranged and in order, yet have encountered one obstacle after another. Thinking Phoenix was a long distance from Sedona, I arranged to fly to Flagstaff and drive to Sedona from there. Now I know this was not necessary and am beginning to feel the panic churning inside as I board a very small commuter plane.

As I fly from Phoenix to Flagstaff in this poor excuse for an airplane, sealed in a small tomb for thirty minutes with fifteen other people, the feeling of being completely out of control overtakes me and tears fill my eyes. Thoughts of solid ground fill my mind. I realize I have felt solid ground only a few times in my life. Being your mother was one of them. And at times it was not unlike riding in an airplane; sometimes crash landing and sometimes soaring with the wonder of you; feeling enriched by the knowledge that I brought life to someone such as you, my son. (*And other times finding it hard to believe you could have! Remember my double Mohawk haircut mom and the call from the police at three a.m.?!*) Yes, and I sense you loving this horrifying flight and laughing all the way. My sense of hu-

Searching

mor did not accompany me. Even when the pilot announced upon landing, "Well, we made it again!" *(The fact you are not taking care of your body doesn't help. Eat, mom.)*

May 20

I wonder what they are thinking? What plays on their minds? Those others whom you touched so harshly with your suicide. Is it consuming them? Do they ever think of you? Am I going crazy alone? (*Well, mom, you're pulled off the side of the road on your way to Williams' Arizona writing in this notebook with tears blinding you. What would be your guess?)*

and then there was one

At the Bright Angel Hotel

May 21

I am on my way to the Grand Canyon on engine 318 of the Grand Canyon Railroad. We were just entertained by a cowboy singer. I reflect that I did not take you many places – long trips – as you were growing up. I allowed life to trick me into the belief that keeping busy with work, the house, etc., was the way to be a "good mother/provider." (*It's hard to be with you sometimes, mom. You seem to have different memories than I do.*) Not surprising. We disagreed about a lot of stuff, especially in your teen years. (*And remember, I wouldn't go places with "my mom" after age 12 without an argument. It just wasn't cool. By the way – did you notice how you are not present in your body right now? Get back in the train and enjoy yourself!*)

Later – still on the train

There are so many things you never did. Never saw the Grand Canyon, never married, never held your baby in your arms, never wrote your novel. (*Not this time, mom – remember I did what I did. Every life is a lifetime.*) Letting go of my wants and wishes for "our life" is difficult. I have to do that before I can decide to go on without you. (*You need to find a connection, mom.*) Tell me more. (*It's not mine to tell.*)

༄༅

I have boarded the tour bus. Once again I am in a seat by myself – room for you, Matt. Have you become my Pooka? The driver keeps us entertained and when we stop and get out to see the view it takes my breath away. I expected it would be beyond beautiful, but did not know I would feel its life. The Canyon stands as a reminder to us that it will be here long after our time has passed and allows us, if we choose, to be here, simply be here for a brief time and feel the joy and security of it with no expectations. Time is still, when looking into the Grand Canyon.

༄༅

Back from the tour I stand at the wall overlooking the Canyon at the Bright Angel Hotel. My legs and feet feel like stone as I ground my body in preparation for our flight. With eyes closed I hold your hand and visualize the two of us flying through the Canyon to a certain spot that looks like a pile of rocks with one flat one on top for us to stand on. As I close my eyes and open my mind and heart to soar I am unable to perform "lift off." (*Your heart is too heavy, mom. Let go – the sadness is releasable.*) I prepare again. It takes me three tries and I am flying through the Canyon with you. The wonder of it overcomes me quickly and I return to my body. (*Stubborn as ever!*) Is the sadness becoming my identity? (*Something to think about, isn't it?*) I am going shopping.

Searching

May 22 The day of your birth

    My plans were to be away from our home and memories of other birthdays, so I flew to Sedona, Arizona. Now I sit in my motel room in the early morning wishing I were home. Longing to be near your room and belongings. Hoping to touch those fading memories and recapture familiar smells and energy.
    When I made my reservations, I forgot how difficult being away is for me. It took all morning but I rearranged my plane and car rental schedules so I can leave on Tuesday instead of Wednesday. I will keep busy today driving around and seeing more sights.

May 23

    Before leaving for the airport in Phoenix I did a little more shopping and picked up the leather pouch a craftsman made to hold your ashes. He was not in his shop when I went in. The pouch was sitting on the counter and the woman there gave it to me and I left. It is nothing like he described, glued not stitched and about one third the size I said would be needed. The lesson I am learning is perhaps I am not supposed to keep your ashes.
    What a a hectic and confusing day so far! I am sitting in an airplane traveling to Sacramento. It feels very good to be going home. While in the airport I finally figured out how to use my cellular phone and made my first call to Beth, asking her to pick me up. Of course I got the answering machine!
    The plane has landed in Sacramento, and I sit in the airport waiting for a ride. I made another call and

Sydnee is coming to meet me after work.

The drive home seemed long. It feels wonderful to be here. As we drive up to the house, I notice the roses are dying. I have not paid any attention to the rose garden since your death, but it is the first thing I see when I get home. All of the leaves are falling off the bushes and weeds cover the ground. I change clothes and work out there until dark. Somehow it is very important to bring it back to life. To make it bloom again.

May 24

Much of today was spent unpacking and finishing work with the roses. Your grandpa planted the bushes more than thirty-five years ago and I have only replaced two. They must not die. (*They aren't, mom, and you are coming back to life.*)

May 29

Jim is my forgetting time, but mostly I live in the time of remembering. Remembering that you are gone, Matt, and I probably have to live without you. I want my family to remember you, to talk about you and to include you at least as much as before your death. I feel so alone when they leave you out; don't talk about you. Like at the birthday party. (*You didn't talk about me, either, or about your trip. Maybe they need you to start. To make it okay for them.*) I am outside looking in at the "events." Not allowing the connections. When I returned from my trip I knew in my thinking

Searching

brain I am not supposed to die now, but in my emotional brain, in my soul, I know today it is too late. *(Reread my last sentence for May 24.)*

and then there was one

ಐಆ
Avalon

May 30

What is ahead? It is almost summer vacation. Almost one year since you died. I feel the same as I did eleven months ago. (*You have to find your own path to life without me.*) I cannot see it for the tears. *(Stop crying. Get outside your grief and see a new world where you belong. There are many who wait.)* I am going to bed.

May 31

Part of the reason for my trip to Sedona was to find just the right container for your ashes. It did not happen and now I am puzzling over whether to keep them or spread them in "Avalon." That is the title I gave to the piece you wrote about the place you called "the most beautiful spot in the world." Your ashes are the only physical part of you I have left. I want to keep that part with me. I am not ready to let it go. I want our ashes to be mixed and spread together. (*You are getting too morbid, mom.*) You started it.

and then there was one

Avalon
by Matt Williams

    In my opinion the most peaceful and majestic place on Earth is the hillside about a half mile down hill from my father's property in Philo, California. I can still remember the first time I saw it. I was about sixteen years old. My dad woke me up around 8:45 a.m. and said, "Get up Matt, there's something I want to show you." Soon after that we left the house and began to walk down the hill. After walking through the forest for about fifteen minutes we reached a fence. Just past the fence I could see a clearing up ahead. After climbing the fence we proceeded to walk into the most beautiful place on Earth!
    A clearing about a half mile long. It was a rolling green hillside dotted by a few scattered oak trees. It was absolutely stunning. The morning mist was still moving across the meadow, and the late spring sunshine was already out in force. It reminded me of what Avalon, in the King Arthur stories must have looked like. I could picture Morgan le Fey and the faerie people walking around planning trouble for Sir Lancelot.
    There was a giant redwood stump at the side of the hill with a large wooden stake driven into it. It was obviously used as a helicopter marker at one time. As I climbed up on it, I had an overwhelming urge to spread my arms back and jump, letting my soul carry me across the valley. How I envied the turkey vultures, I saw gliding on air streams across the meadow and over the valley. I think at that moment I would have sold my soul to be one of them for just five minutes.

Searching

June 4

In church today during his prayer, Steve said "not to let the terror overtake you." As soon as I entered the sanctuary I could feel the contrast of the lively atmosphere of celebration and the confusion and panic that was encircling me. So many people there today. I am having trouble with crowds again. These are people I love, yet I keep myself so distant from them. The fear is becoming a barrier and is consuming me. "Overtaking me." *(Keep accepting love, mom. Don't shut down again. Don't let your pain take you away.)* Why am I feeling so frightened right now? *(You thought you were alone again)*

I went to see my friend Barb after the service. She has her own self designed barrier protecting her from the feelings of still missing her husband, Bill, and from the possibility that she is "going on" without him and not knowing how she is doing it or why. We talked mostly what people call "small talk." Catching up on what she has been doing and what I have not. I am difficult to be with right now, a reminder to Barb of our pain. This is the first time since your death that I have not been honest with her about what I am feeling.

How do I tell my friends that what I want most is to be with my son? I have not been writing much lately. I am shutting down. Do not feel you here today. Do not want to feel.

There is a great amount of commitment that goes with deciding to feel.

June 6

I was never alive before you, Matt. Now I die a little each day. But the death is taking me bit by bit. I am so confused. (*My death was not thought-out, mom. Your's will be a deliberate slam to everyone you care about. It will destroy me again.*)

June 8

Last night I dreamed I was looking for you again. Searching coffee houses this time. At the end of the dream you came out of a door as I opened it. You were younger than when you died. Your face had the expression I used to see when you felt you had failed in some way – were not "measuring up" to whatever was happening at the time. That look of "not being enough." Of having let yourself down by believing you needed to do what others expected rather than satisfying yourself. I want to dream of you at peace, and happy. (*You saw me worried about you. I cannot be at peace until you are, mom.*) I will be at peace when I am with you, son.

Last year at this time I was planing my trip to go with you to Ft. Bragg and Mendocino. This year I am making other plans to be with you. I am so confused, Matt. One moment in time I want to stop this life and be in spirit with you and the next I have a change of heart, wanting to experience life. But I miss you so much. (*Find me other ways. I am not gone from you. I will be with you when you rock the babies while volunteering at the hospital, and when you go on trips, and during quiet times, and in dreams. I love you, mom. Your sadness is*

killing me all over again.)
It will mean redefining who I am. (*Yes, or rearranging and adding to the definition of a great lady – my mom.*)

June 12

School is out for the summer! I do not remember very much of the first months. However, those last ones were nearly my undoing. Two, perhaps three close colleagues are moving on, to other schools to escape the oppression of the present one. A new beginning will be good for them. I, too, would leave if it were not for my teaching partner, Terry. She has been my anchor and dear friend. The stress of this awful year spelled the end of friendship with two others, although they will still be teaching at the same school. We disagree on what I believe to be some unethical behavior that has gone on this year. I am so glad the school year is over. Perhaps time and talking will mend some of what happened.

June 16

You received another bill from Sacramento City College library today. When are you going to pay that fifty-cent fine you left? They have already spent sixty-four cents to remind you. What they are doing is continuing to remind me of your death. I called and told them I doubted you would be paying the bill and they should get on with other very important business. I received a letter of condolence from the superintendent of my school district. She is a little behind in her correspondence. This incredibly insensitive letter has truly been the climax of a school year filled with examples of an imperceptive and uncaring administration. *(Well, they got you thinking about something besides my death for a while.)*

PART FOUR
Continuing!?

and then there was one

Without You

June 19

    June is ending and July fast approaches. One year – a blink in time. I have been attempting to chronicle how my feelings and reactions have changed over the year. When I go into restaurants now and see young men your age waiting on tables, my heart still misses a beat, but no tears. I can almost walk through the men's department of stores without feeling the pain of your absence. Looking at your picture in the hall gives me a feeling of peace some of the time. I am ready to talk to Jason E. about the last weekend you were home. I want more details about that weekend and am ready to hear them. Sometimes I go all day and do not cry when I think about you. I have not slept with your jacket for weeks.

    Going to the grocery store remains difficult. Everywhere I look, I see your favorite foods. Things I would stock up on when you were coming to visit. Your Vespa scooter is still in the garage along with your weight bench. I sat in the rocking chair with your ashes the other night when I could not sleep. The pitcher of tea remains in the refrigerator. (*That's weird, mom.*) I know. I wonder about it a lot, but cannot seem to throw it away.

The "Fourth of July" weekend is coming up and I am scared. Aunt Sydnee's family will have a big get-together and barbecue, with fireworks, etc. I want no celebrations this year. How do I tell them how much it will hurt if they have a celebration? (*Just tell them. Or let them do it. It's okay with me.*) But it is not okay with me. No celebrating. (*Why? This might be your chance to let go of the mourning. A "setting free" of me and the pain of not having me there anymore. A time to set you free.*) It does not feel like a celebrating kind of thing. It feels empty. (*Well, then you can begin to fill up again with new stuff.*) Not interested. (*Ask for help.*) Ask who? (*Our family. All of us.*) I am going to ask them all to come over here on July 7th. The kids too. I want a remembrance time. I wrote letters to everyone, but have not mailed them yet.

June 20

Tiger has been persistent about going into your room. He is constantly at the door. I finally let him in this evening. There must be a mouse in there.

When I opened the door, memories came flooding out in waves of both joy and despair. This used to be my room when I was a child, shared with your aunt. We had many fun times, many arguments, sister secrets, and some tears. We grew up. She married and I moved in and out of my parents home during my early college years. You and I also shared the room. Moving back in with my mom and dad when I became

Continuing!?

pregnant with you was very difficult. My mother was very upset and did not want to tell anyone, least of all my dad. When he was finally told, he was great about it and very supportive. Just wanted to know when I was getting married! Well, that was not in the plan and he was still okay with it. I stayed with them through the last three months of my pregnancy and for five months after your birth. (*We never talked about this mom.*) I know. There is too much we never did, Matt. You left too soon and with too much unfinished. (*Tell me more.*) I moved into a little duplex downtown and continued college. Grandma and Grandpa took care of you while I was in class and then still later when I was teaching. They adored you, especially your grandpa.

You were six years old when Grandpa died and we came back to live with Grandma to take care of her until her death six months later. I am sorry I did not pay more attention to you and realize how hard it was for you when they died. (*You had your hands full with a new job, two dead parents and a kid to raise.*) That last part – that was the good news. (*It didn't feel like it sometimes.*) I know. We can return in our memories and see so clearly how to do things differently – better, but this stops the looking ahead. I must look at the memories and work through the fog of the "if onlys" and get to the other side of all the pain if I am going to survive your death. (*Just don't stay there too long.*)

June 21

Before I began writing last night, I was lying on my bed in the dark watching T.V. when Tiger came in and jumped on my back. After resting there for a while, he walked over to the side of the bed and stood still, staring toward the wall. He remained in this position, just staring for minutes, not moving a bit. I got up and used my dowsing rods to see if there was any energy in the room. The rods remained closed, signaling no energy, until I came to the place where Tiger was looking and they opened wide. It was then I was told to go and do some writing. I took the rods with me and did the same procedure in the computer room. The rods opened in the area of the computer near a shelf where an angel picture sits, as well as three other areas. I could feel the presence of many spirits. I realize this will sound "crazy" to many people, but I never feel alone when I write. When my writing was complete for the night, I used the rods again to check the energy. They remained closed and I went to bed and fell asleep.

June 23

I dread another year of beginning school, of getting through holidays, of being without you. Beginning another year means deciding to live all the years without you. My year is now measured from July to July rather than January to January. Lately, whenever I am with friends, one question is always with me, yet goes unasked. "Do you think I am going to make it? Do you think I will live through July 7th?" I feel so tem-

Continuing!?

porary, not present, like I'm back in the numbness of last July. You would have been better at this. You should be the one having to live without me.

June 25

    People are coming tomorrow to pick up the old freezer, washer and dryer and your old stereo. I was cleaning out your room some more and my closet, too. Lots of "stuff" to get rid of. I have been thinking more about the pitcher of tea. If I throw it away, I will be putting a closure to your death. Saying I am ready to go on with a new life. As long as it is still in there, I can hang onto the old one. (*It's getting moldy! The hanging-on and the tea.*)

and then there was one

ಏಓಚ
Moldy Tea

June 29

I met with Beth for coffee this morning. We sat outside the Galleria and talked for almost three hours. She helped me understand what being twenty-four is like for your generation. The uncertainty that surrounds life even when the mind is clear-thinking. She expressed how it probably was for you after taking drugs again that last weekend of your life. Confirming my belief that they did take away your choice to live and confront whatever problems you had, ending them instead in a depression few ever feel so completely.

June 30

The phrase, <u>and then there was one</u>, came into my thoughts tonight. A description of me. One mother left with no child. But I soon realized that was not the meaning at all. It stands for one connection to all beings. A whole – each person not complete without all the others. From the grocery clerk we talk to briefly during the day or a stranger who asks for spare change, to a member of our family. Each has a purpose for being in our lives. Some stay moments while others twenty-three years or more. The time is relevant only to the information received. To withdraw completely is to ignore the whole and remain isolated in the fog of grief. (*Look farther than your grief mom. The "fog" is lifting. Don't get too comfortable with it. You have much to do.*)

July 2

The battle continues. The curiosities of life v.s. the peace of death.

July 4

The whole day and not one tear. Not even a tightening in my throat. Detached again. This is not still happening. People are not celebrating the "Fourth of July" without you. Why would they want to do that? Yet two doors down, your friends sit around a swimming pool doing just that. (*They aren't there because I'm not. They need a reason to get together. To connect. To say we can go on, it was not the end for us.*) It was for me. (*Once again mom, your choice.*) Yes. What I saw today were many people on the road to self destruction. (*How is it you recognized that so easily?*) It has been my path lately too. (*No shit!*)

While talking with your friend, Nick, many things

Continuing!?

started coming together. He knew you well. (*He got off that "self-destruct road" in time.*) Yes, and he has a beautiful family. The kids look so much like him. Now the tears start. I want you home. (*I am home, mom.*) I want you here.

There is an aloneness that cannot be described, only experienced. It cannot be experienced unless you have raised a child and had him die, leaving an empty place inside where he used to be.

1:00 a.m.

It feels like I am traveling in a time machine being sent back to last year, only this time I know what is going to happen. In two more days you will shoot yourself and I will get a phone call and the year will begin all over again. I guess that is why I have become numb again and am fighting for control. It also feels like being in an airplane crash. I know I am going to hit the mountain any minute, I recognize it and feel the decent into it, but have no power over the outcome. I volunteered to make a poster for the church and it was supposed to be done weeks ago. I have put it off, not understanding why until tonight. The task is easy enough, I have all the materials I need. I am resisting making it because it is the only thing I feel I have control of doing or not doing right now. The plane is scheduled to crash July 7th.

July 5

One year ago tonight you drove off, your truck full of furnishings for your new flat and your mind full of pain not talked about. What you showed us that weekend was a young man full of fun and future. I do still remember the last hug and kiss – thank you, God. As you left I could see in your eyes something was troubling you, but you said everything was okay and of course, that is exactly what I wanted to hear. Did you know then that your life was ending soon? *(No mom, not then. I was confused about the weekend. That I could take the drugs again so easily and thought I could stop again just as easily. I was wrong. I'm sorry mom.)* Sorry is not enough. it's not it's not it's not

July 7

I awoke early this morning without having dreams that I can recall. This is the time you lay alone in the closet waiting for someone to find your body. I know your spirit was no longer there, but my heart aches as I feel and imagine my child bleeding and lying cold in that dark place.
The letters were never sent to the family.

July 8

I do not remember today.

The Battle Continues, but the Fog is Lifting

July 9

    This day is calm and quiet, inside and outside of me. There is peacefulness not felt since before you died. Someone asked if it was the feeling of acceptance I was experiencing. I think more a feeling of compliance. I did "survive" the first year, something I had no intention of doing. Did not believe it possible. One does not survive suicide. The surviving happens to you without consent. More unfair life stuff.

    When I hear my sister's voice, look into her eyes and feel her arms around me I know I am still connected to this earth. Through her I am aware of all of our family who is no longer here, mom, dad, Aunt Thelma, you, and many more. She must not be left alone. I will stay a while longer. (*Now about that pitcher of tea, mom, don't you think it's time to let go?*) I am getting ready.

July 11

The tea no longer ferments in the refrigerator. A dear and knowing friend suggested I might use it to nourish the rose garden and other plants in our yard. This releasing feels right to me. Before I dilute it with more water and pour it on the plants outside, does this letting go of it mean I am completely letting go of you? (*No mom, you are letting go of some more of the grief that no longer serves a purpose for you. I will always be with you. Not always in spirit, but always in your mind and heart and soul. We will both be free to go on with our journeys and connect again when it is time.*)

July 16

The fog has lifted. There is a brightness not viewed since your death. (*It is the love you are now accepting from us.*) Explain "us." (*Me and all who are near you.*) What of the unending tears? (*Use your tears to help clear the fog when it returns.*)

I thought I would die this year, and then July 9th came and I felt such peace. I labeled it "compliance," yet knew it was different. Not understanding until today what was happening.

I can stay in the darkness of grief until there is nothing left of me or I can project the light and love I learned from being your mom to those around me. A friend told me it is "my hero's journey" and it is important to tell it. That in the telling there will be healing for many. It is a journey that may show others who have had something or someone they labeled "their life" taken from them, that this is another beginning, not an ending. If we do not experience our pain, we can-

Continuing!?

not fully experience the rest of ourselves. Getting through and beyond this pain is how we get to the other dimension of ourselves, so we are able to see and understand what created the pain. *(You've got it, mom.)* **No beginnings, no ends, continuous oneness.** Thank you, Matt.

EPILOG:

AND NOW?

and then there was one

Redefining Me

Something happens after a year of grieving. The mind has been turned upside down and inside out during these months until this way of "being" feels normal. As the confusion, panic and sadness subside I am left with wondering.

When did the "grieving mother" part of me disappear? I go about my work no longer consumed with thoughts of Matt. I am able to type our journal in readiness for publication and at times, remain unmoved by it – the story of my son's death. What is happening to me? I do not recognize this part of me. This part that is functioning now is totally split off from the emotional rollercoaster I have been on for months. Only at night when I am alone does the familiar "me" surface as I once again touch the feelings of a childless mother. I am no longer drinking or taking pills to get to sleep. Sleep comes easily. It is still a time of escape from not having Matt with me physically. He is sometimes with me in my dreams, and knowing he is always with me in my heart has made this transition possible.

and then there was one

A few months later:

The roller coaster is once again in motion. I am riding closer to the front of it now. No longer in the back seat unable to see what is coming next or unaware of the descent that always caught me off guard. And the curves are usually visible before I reach them.

I know the void Matt left in my life will always remain. There will never be another Matthew Warren Williams to light that darkness. I will stop pretending this part of me will "heal." I now know the only way I can go forward is with the acceptance of a new definition of me. A woman who knows what it was like to be a mother and lose that part of her forever. My friends say I am still a mother, and death does not change that. My reality tells me I am now a person with memories of mothering, and I am as complete as I allow myself to be.

ORDER FORM

To: Pooka Publishing Company
P.O. Box 19736
Sacramento, California 95816
Or call 916-457-8380

Please send_____copy(ies) of **and then there was one.** I am enclosing $12.95 plus $2.00 postage and handling for each copy.

Subtotal ($12.95 x no. of copies)   _____
California residents add 7.75% sales tax   _____
Postage and handling not to exceed
  $8.00 if all copies are sent to the
  same address   _____

Total amount   _____

Send _____ copy(ies)

NAME   _____
ADDRESS _____
CITY, STATE, ZIP _____

Send _____ gift copy(ies) to:

NAME_____
ADDRESS_____
CITY, STATE, ZIP _____

From:
NAME_____
ADDRESS_____
CITY, STATE, ZIP _____

NOTE: _____
      _____

A REQUEST FROM THE AUTHOR

    The connections between a pet and the grieving process is as varied and unique as the pet itself. You, the readers, have read of my experience with "Tiger" as he reached out to comfort and quell my pain. He continues to "be there" for me when I need to feel an earthly connection to Matt.
    The night before Mother's Day this year (1996), Tiger lay beside me as I slept. It was a night of uneasy sleep. Each time I awoke, his paw was touching me — my arm, cheek, shoulder, as I was lulled back to sleep by his tranquil purring. There is a definite difference in the character of my cat at these times, compared to his "regular" cat behavior.
    I would appreciate hearing of your experiences with pets during times of illness or the death of a loved one. These creatures, who offer unconditional love at times when it is needed the most, sometimes act as channels for spirits to visit. Please tell me if you have also experienced this unique phenomenon by writing to:

Margo Williams
Pooka Publishing Company
P.O. Box 19736
Sacramento, CA 95816